The American Empirical Movement in Theology

American University Studies

Series VII
Theology and Religion
Vol. 70

PETER LANG
New York • Bern • Frankfurt am Main • Paris

Delores Joan Rogers

The American Empirical Movement in Theology

PETER LANG
New York • Bern • Frankfurt am Main • Paris

Library of Congress Cataloging-in-Publication Data

Rogers, Delores Joan
    The American empirical movement in theology /
Delores Joan Rogers.
      p. cm. — (American university studies. Series VII,
Theology and religion ; vol. 70)
      Includes bibliographical references.
      1. Empirical theology—History of doctrines.
2. Meland, Bernard Eugene, 1899-   . 3. Chicago
school of theology—History. 4. Kaplan, Mordecai
Menahem, 1881- . 5. Reconstructionist Judaism—
History. 6. Judaism—United States—Doctrines—
History—20th century. I. Title II. Series: American
university studies. Series VII, Theology and religion ; v. 70.
BT83.53.R64   1990   230'.046—dc20   89-77291
ISBN 0-8204-1218-X   CIP
ISSN 0740-0446

CIP-Titelaufnahme der Deutschen Bibliothek

Rogers, Delores Joan:
The American empirical movement in theology
/ Delores Joan Rogers. – New York; Bern;
Frankfurt am Main; Paris: Lang, 1990.
  (American University Studies: Ser. 7,
  Theology and Religion; Vol. 70)
  ISBN 0-8204-1218-X

NE: American University Studies / 07

© Peter Lang Publishing, Inc., New York 1990

Printed by Weihert-Druck GmbH, Darmstadt, West Germany

Acknowledgment

The influences shaping this book are many and diverse. Though unable to mention all of them, I want to make note of the following outstanding influences as I remember them. First, I must acknowledge the influence of Dr. Carl O. Bangs, whose classes in theology and philosophy whetted my appetite for continued study. Later, the influence of Bernard Meland, both in class and more importantly in *Higher Education and the Human Spirit* was immeasurable. More recently, this book would not have been begun without the encouragement and helpfulness of Dr. Edmund Perry and Dr. Manfred Vogel of the History and Literature of Religions Department of Northwestern University. Each carefully read and criticized the text in its beginning stages and assisted me through many of its revisions. Thomas Derdak, Ph.D. of Peter Lang Publishing, Inc., edited the submitted manuscript and offered helpful suggestions. My friend, The Rev. Marilyn Creel, has undertaken the task of text design, setting the print specifications and preparing the text, tables and index, for publication.

On a less personal level, but equally important, is the help I received from the Spertus College of Judaica Library and its staff, who courteously and helpfully guided me through their excellent selection of books on the development of American Judaism. Northwestern University's vast collection of journals on Mordecai Kaplan made it possible for me to trace the development of Kaplan's thought. Through Northwestern's interlibrary loan office I was able to make contact with and use materials from The Jewish Theological Seminary of America in New York.

Finally, I would add the influence of Ian Barbour, a physicist and theologian. Barbour's *Issues in Science and Religion* informed the final revision of the last chapter. Unfortunately I was introduced to this text too late to make more extensive use of it.

TABLE OF CONTENTS

CHAPTER I

INTRODUCTION

In this book I want to analyze and compare the thought of Mordecai Kaplan and Bernard Meland, two figures within the American Empirical tradition in theology. The American Empirical tradition in theology took seriously that new discoveries and theories in physics, sociology, psychology, and anthropology made a difference in the way in which people understood the universe and their role in it. Kaplan and Meland represent two different ways of speaking theologically within the new world view delineated by modern science. The analysis of their theologies has two areas of concentration. In the first area of concentration, this work intends to show how the thought of Kaplan and Meland illustrates the fact that very different types of theological understanding can arise within empirical theology, broadly understood. A second area of concentration will deal with the influence of their respective religious traditions on the way in which Kaplan and Meland have appropriated and used the empirical material.

In *Our Religious Traditions*, Sterling P. Lamprecht gives an historic analysis of the basic characteristics of Judaism and Protestantism. His thesis is that Judaism is founded on a covenant between God and a corporate entity whereas Protestantism is characterized by an appeal to individual integrity. Lamprecht describes the basic difference in the following ways. He says of Judaism:

Covenant involves more than the persons present at the particular moment when it is first recognized. Its duration is as endless as time is continuous. It embraces successive generations in its bond, unless indeed there be an absolute break in time, so that no legacy is passed on, no results from the past ensue, no continuity of history can be discovered. It means the establishment of a community, a corporate entity, a society of the generations of men.[1]

Of Protestantism he says,

A Protestant...is a man who regards religion as so important that he dare not allow any one else to fashion his opinions for him, but insists upon the right to work out his own salvation for himself. When a Protestant seeks to make explicit the conviction by which he will abide, he naturally comes to protest against the unacceptable restraints of groups which would draw him servilely into conformity with them. He stands apart, sufficient and alone in his individual integrity.[2]

In his book, Lamprecht may have overstated the case, since individual self-fulfillment is not overlooked in Judaism and the Protestant makes a decision within the limits of a given tradition. But it cannot be denied that Judaism is more concerned with the corporate entity, and Protestantism more clearly affirms the importance of the individual believer. In the following analysis of the works of Bernard Meland from the Chicago School of Theology, a Christian, and Mordecai Kaplan, the founder and guiding light of the Reconstructionist movement within Judaism, we will see how these emphases are maintained.

Basic Definitions

The American Empirical movement draws heavily on the thought of James, Dewey, and Whitehead. Randolph Crump Miller, in *The American Spirit in*

Theology, and Bernard Meland in "The Empirical Tradition in Theology at Chicago," have given us a good historical background for this movement.[3] Both Meland and Miller focus on the empirical tradition at Chicago. Undoubtedly this is where the tradition was most strongly developed. However, as I try to make clear in the discussion of Kaplan's thought, the empirical movement in theology was not entirely localized in Chicago.

At the Divinity School of the University of Chicago, the pragmatic school of empiricism stemming from the works of James and Dewey was influential from the 1900s through the 1920s, with Dewey's thought being more important. At the end of the 1920s, and especially with the coming of Henry Nelson Wieman to the Divinity School, until the end of the 1940s, the organismic thought of Whitehead became more important and finally predominated.[4] Although Wieman introduced Whitehead's thought to the Divinity School, Wieman himself, in his theological writings, was much more influenced by Dewey's "emphasis on empirical observation and verification."[5] James's influence was most pronounced in the works of Gerald Birney Smith in the 1920s, and James's influence continued strongly in the work of Bernard Meland.[6] In Meland's thought we have a synthesis of Jamesian and Whiteheadian influences.

From the writings of these philosophical thinkers—James, Dewey, and Whitehead—two basic assumptions about the nature of empirical data are gleaned. The first assumption is that empirical data is always relational and contextual. There are no isolated data of the senses in the Humean sense. John Dewey describes the relational structure of experience in the following manner:

> The old center was mind knowing by means of an equipment of powers complete within itself, and merely exercised upon an antecedent external material equally complete in itself. The new center is indefinite interactions taking place within a course of

nature which is not fixed and complete, but which is capable of
direction to new and different results through the mediation of
intentional operations. Neither self nor world, neither soul nor
nature (in the sense of something isolated and finished in its
isolation) is the center, any more than either earth or sun is the
absolute center of a single universal and necessary frame of
reference. There is a moving whole of interacting parts; a center
emerges wherever there is effort to change them in a particular
direction.[7]

Another statement about the relational character of existence emerges in
Whitehead's analysis of "causal efficacy" and "presentational immediacy."
Presentational immediacy is roughly equivalent to Hume's isolated data of the
senses. Causal efficacy is the mode of perception that directly perceives the
structure of past relations from the point of view of a present given focus.
Causal efficacy is the impress of the past on the present. Whitehead comes to
the conclusion:

...that the perceptive mode of presentational immediacy arises in
the later originative phases of the process of concrescence. The
perceptive mode of causal efficacy is to be traced to the constitution of the datum by reason of which there is a concrete per-
cipient entity. Thus we must assign the mode of causal efficacy to
the fundamental constitution of an occasion so that in germ this
mode belongs even to organisms of the lowest grade; while the
mode of presentational immediacy requires the more sophisticated
activity of the later stages of process, so as to belong only to
organisms of a relatively high grade.

Whitehead concludes, "It must be remembered that clearness in consciousness
is no evidence for primitiveness in the genetic process: the opposite doctrine
is more nearly true."[8]

One never sees isolated drops of experience but always relational data.
One sees chairs, tables, and even these within a context of diminishing
relevance. From the perspective of the American Empirical movement there

are no isolated data of the senses and no simple ideas except as abstractions from the relational flux.[9]

The second assumption is that meaning, value, and significance are immanent, that is, within the historical, temporal flux. Grace and goodness, as well as evil and destruction, are part of the matrix within which we exist.[10]

The Typology

Within this general definition of empirical, three distinct types of theology can be recognized, which I have designated the functional, the rational, and the mystical types. My reason for using this terminology throughout the text is that it simplifies and makes clearer from an empirical standpoint just what is methodologically important in the theologies in question. Theologies such as Wieman's and Kaplan's, which draw on the work of John Dewey as their base, are often described as "empirical" in comparison to the "radical empiricism" of William James or Gerald Birney Smith. Theologies based on Dewey model themselves after the research methods of modern science and particularly the social sciences. As in a laboratory experiment, the function or action of a process is studied to see what it does in the situation. The emphasis is not on discrete data in the Humean sense but on how processes change under differing circumstances. The attempt is made to isolate relational variables in order to understand their effect on other variables. Since the emphasis is on abstracting a process from the total perceptual complex in order to determine what it does or how it functions, I think it simplifies matters to speak of this type of empirical theology as functional rather than empirical since "radical empiricism" or "empirical realism" as well as process thought intend to begin from an empirical base.[11]

Following the suggestion of Bernard Meland that Gerald Birney Smith's theology and his own could be classified as mystical, I have used that term instead of "radical empiricism" or "empirical realism"[12] because it picks up what I consider to be the most distinguishing characteristic of Meland's thought. This mystical type of theologizing attempts to take into account the total relational field of an entity which includes for human beings an awareness of God. This insistence on being aware of the total relational field is illustrated in James's essay on the mind. Here James makes it clear that he is not intending to study abstractions from the totality of the mind.

> We now begin our study of the mind from within. Most books start with sensations, as the simplest mental facts, and proceed synthetically, constructing each higher stage from those below it. But this is abandoning the empirical method of investigation. No one has ever had a simple sensation by itself.[13]

Just as one does not understand mind on the basis of simple sensation, so one does not understand human experience unless one includes that which is beyond human existence. In its broadest limits, human experience includes the other or the divine for James. There is within experience "a personality lying outside our own and other than us,—a power not ourselves."[14] This other can never be assimilated into human consciousness. Ultimately God is that mysterious other to which human's respond but that response never results in an identity of the human and the divine. As James says,

> In every being that is real there is something external to, and sacred from, the grasp of every other. God's being is sacred from ours. To cooperate with his creation by the best and rightest response seems all he wants of us. In such cooperation with his purposes, not in any chimerical speculative conquest of him, not in any theoretic drinking of him up, must lie the real meaning of our destiny.[15]

By using the term mystical, this text is emphasizing that certain theologies display an attitude toward life that "reverses the discursive and analytical approach."[16] These theologies attempt within an empirical framework to be open to reality as a whole.[17] The theologian who is a naturalistic mystic sees life in the following terms:

> He envisages the world with a scope and a fullness that far exceed the circumscribed perspective of the activist or the discursive thinker who, of necessity, thinks within narrowly defined environings. The insight of the mystic, therefore, is the insight that comes with the approach of openness and wide receptivity.[18]

A mystical theology emphasizes the depth and mystery of existence that goes beyond human comprehension.[19]

The rational type refers to those within the broad understanding of empirical theology who emphasize metaphysical or ontological considerations.[20] This type of theology has as its major concern the structure of experience; and the emphasis is on coherence, on a rational grasp of the whole, the whole of experienced reality. As will be noted later in this book, rational in this context has a this-worldly connotation. It is not concerned with an ideal sphere but with the structure of experience within the natural world. With this basic typology in mind we can go on to a fuller description of the basic categories.

1.   The Functional Strand

Within this category, the emphasis is on how things work, or on how to set goals and predict the results. What function does a certain body of data have within a given system, or what needs to be done to produce a certain function? The emphasis is on what is manageable and what can be clearly defined within a social context. Mordecai Kaplan is representative of this functional emphasis within Empirical Theology. This functional approach seeks clarity— it attempts to isolate specific structures and definable or manageable processes within the world and society.[21]

John Dewey is of special importance for those who seek to do theology within a functional framework. The early Chicago School was dominated by Dewey. Under his influence, "environmental influence and functional adaptation"[22] were emphasized. "Empiricism in this context was thus a study of the functional aspect of phenomena. A thing or movement was known in terms of the function it served."[23]

For Dewey, the divine or God is a functional term and refers both to ideal possibilities and to all the natural forces that combine to bring this ideal about. He typically speaks of the idea of God in the following way.

> This idea is, as I have said, one of ideal possibilities unified through imaginative realization and projection. But this idea of God, or of the divine, is also connected with all the natural forces and conditions—including man and human association—that promote the growth of the ideal and that further its realization.[24]

Those theologies which follow Dewey's mode of reasoning tend to focus on God as that function or instrument in human affairs that increases human good. Henry Nelson Wieman exemplifies this type of theologizing when he says,

> We shall try to demonstrate that there is a creative process working in our midst which transforms the human mind and the world relative to the human mind. We shall then show how transformation by this process is always in direction of greater good. The human good thus created includes goods, satisfaction of human wants, richness of quality, and power of man to control the course of events.[25]

Theology, in this mode, concerns itself with values and ethics. Theology is no longer relegated to tangential concerns but becomes a science concerned with determining those forces within the human community and in the larger environment that promote human good. Theology becomes a practical tool for revitalizing social groups and for making life for the individual within the group more fulfilling and worthwhile. A practical and reforming spirit emanates from this understanding of the role of theology. The Divinity School under the influence of Shailer Mathews and Edward Scribner Ames exemplified this spirit.[26] Similarly, in Kaplan's case, this mode of theologizing issued in plans for reforming Jewish education, a design for Jewish Community Centers, guidelines for Jewish Social Work, and liturgical reforms that helped reinforce these innovations.[27]

The theologians within this group may be aware of the complexity and depth of the relational flux, but the emphasis on function leads them to name as God only that aspect of the relational field that has instrumental value, *i.e.*, only that which promotes the growth of the ideal and that furthers its realization. Thus, it can be said that this functional approach to theology distorts the empirical data in the direction of simplicity, that it ignores the depth and texture of experience and gains clarity for its functional purpose at the expense of profundity.

2.   The Rational Strand

A second strand within empirical theology is the rational one. A detailed analysis of a major figure within this group will not be given within this text, but since one cannot understand either the functional or the mystical emphasis

without referring to the rational (and throughout this text references will be
made to the rational), a short explication will be given here.

The rationalists within the empirical movement build a superstructure of
logic that at times obscures their empirical base, but even the most rational
among them, *i.e.*, Charles Hartshorne, begin with lived experience and try to
provide the necessary structure that makes such lived experience possible.
Even Hartshorne's famous ontological argument receives its validity because it
is a way of making sense out of the "concrete God at work in contingent
events and by the intuitions of faith."[28] The concrete lived experience of
human beings not only forms the basis from which all speculative ventures
begin, but is also that to which all speculation must return for verification and
for new insights. Whitehead speaks to this point in the following way:

> The true method of discovery is like the flight of an aeroplane. It
> starts from the ground of particular observation; it makes a flight
> in the thin air of imaginative generalization; and it again lands for
> renewed observation rendered acute by rational interpretation.[29]

The rationalist school includes Charles Hartshorne, to whom reference
was made above, and his younger students and colleagues from the University
of Chicago Divinity School, John Cobb and Schubert Ogden. This school of
thought is less troubled by the notion of relativity than are either Kaplan or
Meland. In Whiteheadian terms, they underplay that each individual prehension is always from a particular perspective and they see a greater correlation
between human and Divine reason. They tend to see metaphysical structures
as more than tentative attempts to give coherence and unity to felt experience;
they see metaphysical structures as descriptive of ultimate reality in a rather
literal sense. Meland, on the other hand, feels deeply that there is no prehend-
ing stance that would allow an individual to ascertain the structure of the

whole, and Kaplan excludes metaphysical concerns in his theological enterprise.

3.   The Mystical Strand

It is the emphasis on mystery and on the richness and depth of lived experience that goes beyond what the rational or empirical method can discern which separates the mystic from both the functionalists and the rationalists. The term "mystical naturalism" was first used by one of Meland's mentors at the University of Chicago, Gerald Birney Smith. Smith, as Randolph Crump Miller in *The American Spirit in Theology* has pointed out, was an oddity within the Divinity School ethos.[30] During a period of modernism in which the majority of his colleagues were devoted to religious humanism, Smith, in the words of Bernard Meland, set himself "to discovering whether the natural universe as described by the sciences, was hostile to a religious response and a doctrine of theism."[31] Modernism at The Divinity School, especially under Shailer Mathews, focused on the religious meaning and values of the Church community. Smith was out of step with the majority of his colleagues when he raised the question that appears as the title of an article in *The American Journal of Theology*, "Is Theism Essential to Religion."[32] The question might have seemed irrelevant for his colleagues, but Smith was convinced that the answer had to be affirmative if religion were to survive.

Smith was also convinced that if the theistic position was to be defended in our modern world, then a radical new way of talking about the divine had to be inaugurated. The old traditional, static categories used by theologians of the past to describe God needed to be replaced by categories and ideas that were adequate to deal with the kind of world described by modern science. He was pleased therefore when his colleague at the Divinity School, Henry Nelson Wieman, produced *Religious Experience and Scientific Method*. Smith saw this work as an attempt to take science seriously within a theological framework. However, he was also of the opinion that theological method had to do more than duplicate scientific method. Theology needed to take into account the full impact of human experience. The theologian's method should be closer to that of the poet than to the method of the scientist, because the poet is sensitive to the nuances and depths of experience that are completely ignored by the scientist. For Smith, the goal was symbolic formulation, not scientific expression. In a review of *Religious Experience and Scientific Method*, he said, "The creative power of religion depends fundamentally on the possibility of feeling the reality of what has not been precisely formulated by science."[33]

This perception of that which cannot be strictly defined is basic to Smith's understanding of what is meant by the term "mystical naturalism." Mystical, in this sense, does not describe an out-of-time experience, or a level of reality beyond the natural order. Rather, it describes an attitude of being attentive to that within the natural cosmos which upholds and supports human values. This attentiveness is aimed not so much at detailed meanings but at the richness and depth of any given moment.[34]

Smith died before he could articulate a fully developed position, but it is clear what direction he thought theology should go. He argued that theologians of the future should be attentive to the data provided by the empirical, inductive methods of science, but he also maintained that theologians should not neglect developing a sensitivity to the aesthetic and emotional side of life. Theology should be as rigorous as science and philosophy, but ultimately theology is a poetic-philosophical enterprise and not simply an instrumental or rational endeavor.[35]

The mystic wants to stress the fullness and complexity of life that goes beyond all attempts at complete definition and systematization. He accedes that the functional and rational approaches have validity within limits or perimeters, but he wants to be attentive to what William James has called the "More" in existence.[36]

The basic criticism of mystical naturalism is that it could lead to the abandonment of the search for objective truth. It can be said that the attempt to give due weight to that which is non-rational and mysterious in existence is both its strength and weakness.

CHAPTER I, NOTES

1. Sterling P. Lamprecht, *Our Religious Traditions*. (Cambridge: Harvard University Press, 1980) 11.

2. Ibid., 1.

3. Randolph Crump Miller, *The American Spirit in Theology* (Philadelphia: United Church Press, 1974); Bernard E. Meland, "The Empirical Tradition in Theology at Chicago," *The Future of Empirical Theology* (Chicago: The University of Chicago Press, 1969) 1–62.   Additional information about empirical theology at Chicago can be obtained from Larry E. Axel, "The Chicago School of Theology and Henry Nelson Wieman," *Encounter* 40 (Autumn 1979): 341–358.   For additional information about the movement from the point of view of Whitehead's philosophy see Delwin Brown and Gene Reeves, "The Development of Process Theology," *Process Philosophy and Christian Thought* (New York: Bobbs-Merrill Co., Inc., 1971) 23–69.

4. Cf. Meland, "Empirical Tradition in Theology," 5.

5. Brown and Reeves, "Development of Process Theology," 25.

6. Cf. Miller, *American Spirit in Theology*, 64–65.   A fuller explication of the "Early Chicago School" and its impact on Bernard Meland is included in this work in the section on "Formative Influences."

7. John Dewey, *The Quest for Certainty* (New York: G. P. Putnam's Sons, 1929) 291.

8. Alfred North Whitehead, *Process and Reality* (1929; New York: The Free Press, 1969) 200 and 201.

9. Cf. Ibid., 78.

10. Cf. Bernard M. Loomer, "Empirical Theology within Process Thought," *The Future of Empirical Theology* (Chicago: University of Chicago Press, 1969) 151–158.

11. Cf. William Dean, "Radical Empiricism and Religious Art," *Journal of Religion* 61 (April 1981): 168; Nancy Frankenberry, "Meland's Empirical Realism and the Appeal to Lived Experience," *American Journal of Theology and Philosophy* 5 (May and September, 1981): 116–129; Bernard Meland, "In Response to Frankenberry," *American Journal of Theology and Philosophy* 5 (May and September, 1981): 134–135; and Bernard Meland, "Can Empirical Theology Learn from Phenomenology," *The Future of Empirical Theology*, 285.

12. Cf. Bernard Meland, "In Response to Miller," *American Journal of Theology and Philosophy*, 5 (May and September 1981): 109; Henry Nelson Wieman and Bernard Meland, *American Philosophies of Religion* (Chicago: Willett, Clark and Co., 1936) 291–295; and Bernard Meland, *Modern Man's Worship* (New York: Harper and Bros., 1934) xi.

13. William James, *The Principles of Psychology*, 2 vols. (1890, New York: Dover Publications, Inc., 1950) vol. 1, 224.

14. William James, *Essays on Faith and Morals* (1962, New York: The World Publishing Co., 1968) 134.

15. Ibid., 141.

16. Wieman and Meland, *American Philosophies of Religion*, 292.

17. Cf. Ibid., 291–292.

18. Ibid., 293.

19. In *American Philosophies of Religion*, Bernard Meland and Henry Nelson Wieman provide the category of "Mystical Naturalism" under the larger rubric of "Empirical Theists." Ibid., 291–295. My category is simply an abridgement of the one they proposed, since to speak of empirical presupposes naturalism.

20. Cf. Charles Hartshorne, *Man's Vision of God* (1941; Hamden Court—Archer Books, 1964); Hartshorne, *The Logic of Perfection* (LaSalle, IL: Open Court Publication Co., 1964); and Miller, *American Spirit in Theology*, 164–166.

21. Cf. Bernard Meland, *Realities of Faith* (New York: Oxford University Press, 1962) 105.

22. Meland, "Empirical Tradition in Theology," 18.

23. Ibid., 18.

24. John Dewey, *A Common Faith* (1934; New Haven: Yale University Press, 1969) 50.

25. Henry Nelson Wieman, *The Source of Human Good* (Carbondale, IL: Southern Illinois University Press, 1946) 17.

26. Cf. Meland, "Empirical Tradition in Theology," 18.

27. Cf. Samuel Dinn, "Organic Jewish Community," *Mordecai M. Kaplan: An Evaluation* (New York: Jewish Reconstructionist Foundation, 1952) 45–64; Other papers from the same volume that develop on the theology of social reform include, Samuel C. Kohs, "Jewish Social Work," 65–87; Louis Kraft, "The Jewish Center Movement," 119–136; David Polish, "Jewish Liturgy," 211–222. For detail on the liturgical innovations envisioned see *High Holiday Prayer Book* 2 vols., (1948; New York: Jewish Reconstructionist Foundation, 1951). Both volumes were edited by a team including Mordecai Kaplan.

28. Miller, *American Spirit in Theology*, 166.

29. Whitehead, *Process and Reality*, 7. Cf. Meland, "Empirical Tradition in Theology," 54.

30. Miller, *American Spirit in Theology*, 60–61.

31. Meland, *Future of Empirical Theology*, 8.

32. Gerald Birney Smith, "Is Theism Essential to Religion?" *American Journal of Theology* 24 (January, 1920): 153.

33. Miller, *The American Spirit in Theology*, 61, and Gerald Birney Smith, "Religious Experience and Scientific Method," *Journal of Religion* 6 (November, 1926): 638–640.

34. Cf. Wieman and Meland, *American Philosophies of Religion*, 291–293.

35. Cf. Miller, *American Spirit in Theology*, 62–64.

36. Cf. Meland, "Empirical Tradition in Theology," 25.

CHAPTER II

MORDECAI KAPLAN

Formative Influences

1. Jewish Theological Seminary

Mordecai Kaplan is a pioneer and innovator within Judaism. Unlike Bernard Meland, Mordecai Kaplan felt he could not build on the insights and basic notions presented by his teachers. Whereas Meland saw his work as an unfolding and continuation of the work his teachers had begun, Kaplan saw his work as essentially in conflict with the basic understandings of his teachers. When Kaplan entered the Jewish Theological Seminary in 1893, it was a bastion of traditionalist thinking. According to Herbert Parzen in *Architects of Conservative Judaism*, a history of The Jewish Theological Seminary and the Conservative movement in Judaism, the seminary under Dr. H. Periera Mendes and Dr. Sabato Morais reflected the influence of the extreme right wing of the Conservative Movement.

> The Seminary program, as conceived by these men, regarded Jewish law as authoritative and binding. It sought to train a Rabbinate secularly educated and learned in Rabbinics, devout and loyal to Israel's traditions. Implicitly it rejected Higher Criticism.[1]

Both Dr. Mendes and Dr. Morais frowned on any departure from traditional practice in the synagogues.

The traditionalism of its leaders was reflected in the classrooms. As Kaplan remembers it, at the same time he was being introduced to theories of evolution and modern science's picture of the universe as self-enclosed at City College of New York and later at Columbia, his classes in the Seminary were concentrating on the world-view presented by medieval Jewish philosophers. In the light of his understanding of the modern world, Kaplan found the understanding of Judaism derived from the medievalists woefully inadequate. As he says, "The study of the Jewish medieval philosophers, which was part of the Seminary curriculum, did not help to bridge the gap that divided the thought world of the Bible and the Talmud from the thought world I lived in."[2]

Kaplan lamented the fact that, for the medieval Jewish philosophers and for his teachers at the Seminary, the Bible spoke an eternal language. There was no concept of development nor any place for understanding historical context.

> From first to last those theologians were devoid of any historical
> sense or of any conception of evolution in religion. How could
> they possibly satisfy me, when whatever I studied had to have for
> me its own intrinsic context in order to have meaning?[3]

Kaplan felt that his teachers had no understanding of truth as process. For them, truth did not arise out of the data of the experienced world nor from historical situations or change. Truth was static and complete, or at the most truth in a particular situation was the making explicit of what was already implicit in the original revelation. Details of authorship, dates, and the historical context surrounding the Biblical texts were irrelevant. History was finally unimportant, because the real focus of truth was not to be found there but in an eternal realm.[4]

Faced with this utter disregard for modern ideas and methods of scholarship, Kaplan was forced to go outside the seminary for ways to reconcile his "Jewish consciousness" with his understanding of the modern world.

2.   Biblical Exegesis

From 1894 until 1906, during and after his studies at the seminary and ordination, which took place in 1902, Kaplan studied the Bible with a noted scholar and old friend of the family, Arnold Ehrlich. Ehrlich, whom Kaplan referred to as "one of the greatest Jewish exegetes in modern times,"[5] was a noted textual critic. More than that however, he insisted on studying the Bible in order to find out what it meant for the original authors of the text. In Kaplan's words, Ehrlich was

> the greatest Bible expositor among Jews in modern times. Ehrlich opened up to me that appreciation of the Bible which has enabled me to read it as the expression of the spiritual genius of Israel, and which revealed to me the intrinsic depth and beauty of the original meaning of the text.[6]

Ehrlich's impact on Kaplan was enormous, partly because Kaplan's growing disenchantment with traditional teachings made him receptive to the radical ideas being presented. In speaking of his teacher, Kaplan says:

> He taught me to penetrate through the vast layers of traditional commentaries to the rock-bottom original intent of the biblical authors. In doing so, he undermined my belief in the Mosaic authorship of the Torah and in the historicity of the miracles.[7]

Ehrlich's influence on Kaplan then was both positive and negative. Along with the tearing down and destruction of traditional understandings, there was also engendered in Kaplan an appreciation of the original historical situation and an appreciation of the meaning that the texts had in the time when they were written.

3.   Sociology and Pragmatism

Kaplan's search to maintain his own integrity as a Jewish religious teacher and a modern scholar led him in turn to the writings of Emile Durkheim, William James, and John Dewey for clues as to how to reconceive the religious dimension of life. As Kaplan saw it, this reconception was not only his individual concern but was a concern that was vitally necessary if Judaism was not to lose the brightest and most thoughtful of its young people. He undertook to reconceive religion not to reduce the importance of the Jewish religion, but in order to make religion a viable option for the cultured and educated Jew.[8]

In *The Religion of Ethical Nationhood,* he notes the similarity between his own intellectual journey and that of Susanne K. Langer, author of *Philosophy in a New Key.* Ms. Langer noted that when she began to have faith in her own intellectual powers and the ability of her own mind to reason, she found religion dispensable. Kaplan also found that he was beginning to have more faith in his own mind than in the Orthodox Jewish tradition in which he had been raised and educated. He did not follow Ms. Langer in her rejection of religion, however. The impact of modern thought did not lead him to reject the values within traditional religion. Nonetheless, the impact of modern thought did lead him to rethink some of the traditional beliefs. He concluded, "I decided to leave the Orthodox rabbinate, not Judaism."[9]

From that time onward, Kaplan saw his attempt to understand "Judaism as the evolving religious civilization of the Jewish people"[10] as a religious task. By conceiving of Judaism and Judaism's God as evolving entities, he sought to make Judaism and religion a viable option for the Jew perplexed by the conflict between the modern world and the traditional understanding of the world. He began his reinterpretation, which eventually developed into the Reconstructionist movement, as an attempt to help others like himself who could not be satisfied with being merely secular Jews.[11] For those Jews who could not find a home within the then-existing denominations within Judaism, Kaplan hoped to offer a plausible version of Judaism, one that maintained the traditional values and yet faced up to the realities of the modern world.

Kaplan understood the realities of the modern world as necessitating a naturalistic world view, and that religion must conform to the naturalistic and scientific insights of the modern world. He maintains that this is as true of our understanding of God as it is for all other aspects of religion. "Our conception of God must be self-consistent and consistent with whatever else we hold to be true."[12] The term God cannot be understood as an exception to principles held to be universally valid. Thus God cannot be outside the natural system. God cannot be a mysterious other that exists and acts in ways that are contradictory to the way the rest of the system works. It is a basic tenet for Kaplan that "whatever we say or think about God shall be in harmony with all else that we hold to be true."[13] This leads him to the conclusion that "we cannot, for example, believe that God performs miracles, and at the same time believe in the uniformities of the natural law demanded by scientific theory."[14] The scientific world view determines the boundaries within which religion and God must be understood.

The French sociologist Emile Durkheim provided Kaplan with material that was to aid him in his reconstruction of religion. This reconstruction was to find its basis not in metaphysics or philosophical speculation not even in revelation, but in social-behavior or social-psychology. "The only alternative to the traditional and supernaturalist conception of God's self-manifestation that can make a difference in people's lives is not the metaphysical approach but the social-behavioral one."[15] Religion is not the result of some divine revelation but grows out of the organic unity and value system of a given group. It was from Durkheim that he learned to think of religion as that by which the organic unity of a group, a nation, or a clan was symbolized. According to Durkheim, the unity of a group was symbolized by gods who were conceived of as being interested in the welfare of the group.[16] Even religious rites and festivals aided in the development of group consciousness. They did this by focusing on the social aspects of existence; *i.e.*, by re-enacting the traditional history of the group, by re-emphasizing its moral system and by re-calling the group's cosmology.

In *Judaism as A Civilization,* the first of his major works, Kaplan quotes the following passage from *Elementary Forms of the Religious Life.* During festival time the people's

> thoughts are centered upon their common beliefs, their common traditions, the memory of their great ancestors, the collective ideal of which they are the incarnation; in a word, upon social things. Even the material interests which these great religious ceremonies are designed to satisfy concern the public order and are therefore social. Society as a whole is interested that the harvest be abundant, that the rain fall at the right time and not excessively, that the animals reproduce regularly. So it is society that is in the foreground of every consciousness; it dominates and directs all conduct; that is equivalent to saying that it is more living and active, and consequently more real, than in profane times.[17]

Not only does the worship of the group's gods provide for the unity of a society, the focus also allows for the notion of continuity. "Who are we?" is answered in terms of social identity, symbolized by the god or gods. "Where did we come from?" is likewise a question answered by reference to the gods. Continuity and history come about according to Kaplan's analysis in the following manner. The gods of a people were thought of as immortal, beginning in the remote past and continuing into the future. "Thus it was through the medium of the gods that the individual grew aware of his people, not only as a group existing in the present, but as one whose life extended far into the past, and was expected to endure eternally."[18]

Following Durkheim, Kaplan is led to believe that those groups survived in the evolutionary process and achieved a civilized state when individuals of those societies learned to identify their own interests and well-being with the survival of the group.

> In any society, group solidarity is contingent upon the degree to which the individual identifies his own interests and well-being with the interests and well-being of the group to which he belongs. As soon as a considerable number of individuals begin to sense a conflict between their interests and those of the group disintegration of the group has set in.[19]

Religion helps reinforce this notion of the group's paramount importance through its ideals, customs, and traditions. Even religious doctrines and dogmas are not expressions of metaphysical truths so much as notions that serve to consolidate the group and emphasize its importance.

The importance of the group leads to the notion that the individual can only achieve salvation within the group. Kaplan accepts the idea that the supreme importance of the group means "that one's people will always constitute one's chief source of salvation, and therefore one's chief medium of religion."[20] Salvation is not an otherworldly concept for Kaplan. Salvation is individual self-fulfillment within a given section of humankind that constitutes the individual's own special folk. He points out that in the Jewish Religion, "the requirement of membership in Israel is a prerequisite to salvation."[21] For Kaplan, the sacredness of a people depends on its ability to provide salvation or self-fulfillment for its members. By substituting this Durkheimian notion of

self-fulfillment as only being possible through one's own group for the older
Jewish notion of election, Kaplan was able to maintain the importance of the
Jewish people.[22] He saw it as "the inescapable law of human nature that only
through interaction with his group can the individual achieve personality and
self-fulfillment or salvation."[23] The group about which Kaplan is most concerned, the Jewish people, is no longer to be considered as elected by God
for a special task or even to be a special people. The importance of Jewish
survival no longer can be dependent on the traditional idea of election. On the
other hand, if salvation can only be obtained through one's folk group, then
this group—the Jewish people—can still maintain its uniqueness and religious
significance in the modern world. For Kaplan, Durkheim provided a way of
retaining the importance of the Jewish people and a way of understanding that
importance in accordance with a modern world view. Kaplan was at one with
his forefathers in asserting the importance of the Jewish people; he maintained
his integrity as a modern thinker by revising the meaning of that importance.

The above section makes clear that in many respects Kaplan's thought
was dependent on Durkheim's constructions. However, Kaplan saw significant
differences between his understanding of religion and Durkheim's. Durkheim
understood the term God to refer to the projection of humanity's fears,
fantasies, and desires. Kaplan understood God to refer to a real process in
human existence and in the natural world. Religion and culture are inseparable
just as Durkheim had supposed, but there is a transcendent God at work
within a cultural context. "Belief in God is the intuitive experience of cosmic
Power upon which we depend for our existence and self-fulfillment."[24] This
belief in God as a transcendent power or process is the constant factor in
religion. By "transcendent" Kaplan means that there are forces in nature that
go beyond human personality that aid human beings in achieving salvation.

These forces are not beyond nature but are part of the moral structure of the cosmos. In "Naturalism as a Source of Morality and Religion" Kaplan says,

> Divinity is conceived as a correlate of whatever processes, rela-
> tionships, and conditions make for man's salvation. Divinity is
> thus a particular aspect of the cosmos or nature as a whole,
> including man himself.[25]

Divinity is not supernatural nor is it a super-person. The particular concept of God differs among individuals within a given religion according to "variations of temperament, education, and environmental influences."[26] Furthermore, the idea of God differs in accordance with the different stage of development of a given civilization.[27]

Convinced by Durkheim and by his traditional education of the impor-tance of the Jewish people, Kaplan was to find in the Pragmatism of William James a method "of grappling with the problem of Jewish survival."[28] In *Pragmatism,* published in 1928, William James provided the essential meaning of pragmatism. For him a true idea is one that works in the long run.[29] The method for determining between metaphysical options is to determine the practical consequences. The practical consequences are determined by what is possible in the real world. Truth is never a matter of abstraction or definition, but is concerned with what is possible in the context of real human experi-ence. He puts the matter in the following way.

> Pragmatism asks its usual question—"Grant an idea or belief to
> be true," it says, "what concrete differences will its being true
> make in any one's actual life?" ...The truth of an idea is not a
> stagnant property inherent in it. Truth *happens* to an idea. It
> *becomes* true, is *made* true by events. Its verity *is* in fact an
> event, a process, the process made of its verifying itself, its
> verification.[30]

James gives the example of a mountain climber who comes to an abyss. The climber cannot go back and must either cross the abyss or perish. If one truly believes one will get across, the chances are one will. That is the truth for this situation. One's belief that one can jump across is proven to be true by the fact that one survives the jump. The belief that one can make it across the abyss has made a verifiable difference in the way in which the individual acted. James was willing to extend the notion of verifiability far beyond what others who called themselves pragmatists were willing to do. Thus he could say, "God is real since he produces real effects."[31] When human beings commune with the divine, "work is actually done upon our finite personality, for we are turned into new men, and consequences in the way of conduct follow in the natural world upon our regenerative change."[32] For James, just as the mountain climber's belief made a difference in the way the climber acted, belief in God makes a difference in the way in which people act. James goes on to say that the highest conception of God is of God as personal. God is the being to whom individuals can communicate, the being to whom human actions have significance.

Kaplan accepted James's notion that religion had consequences and needs to be verified in life, but his prime concern was not with individual and psychological phenomena, nor with the notion of a personal God. In "How May Judaism be Saved," written in 1916, Kaplan criticizes James for his apparent unawareness that religion is never fully understood if one concentrates on personal or individual experience. Each person's religious experience is closely bound up with the kind of group of which the person is a member. As Kaplan says:

> Evidently, the religious experience of the individual is closely bound up with the general life about him. To pass over this relation as James does by a casual allusion to suggestion and imitation, is to overlook the fact that religion as a complete

reality is to be thought of in connection only with a group and not with an individual. Even where the experiences seem most personal and entirely isolated from the environment, as is the case with visions, trances, hallucinations, a closer examination will inevitably reveal the operation of social forces generated by the religious life of the group to which the highly sensitized individual belongs.[33]

James's investigations into religious experience led him to the conclusion that there was a wider self, which James understood as a "personal other" who related to humanity. However, Kaplan rejects the notion of a personal other in favor of understanding the "wider self" as group consciousness. He argues against James's conclusion that there is a personal, transcendent other: "But what is this *wider self*? Instead of answering *the social mind*, he suddenly transports us into another dimension of existence from the sensible and merely *understandable* world."[34] Kaplan concludes,

How much better we would have fared if he had taken us by the hand at this juncture and helped us explore the true "wider self" through which saving experiences come, the *group consciousness* which is a means to the sense of exhilaration and triumph that we term salvation.[35]

In "The Relation of Religion to Social Life," Kaplan makes his meaning very clear. "The belief in an invisible order arises from the experience of an invisible order. That invisible order is the soul of the group, the collective will which cannot be seen or touched but which binds and compels the individual as surely as chains and lashes."[36]

Since he found in James's analysis of the human situation a tendency to ignore the importance of the social dimension, he turned to another pragmatist, John Dewey, for further insight on how to understand the function of religion as a group phenomenon and an individual's religion as arising out of his identification with the group. As William Kaufman says, "Kaplan found James's version of pragmatism lacking because it did not sufficiently stress the social character of truth and the role of social conditioning in religious experience."[37] For Dewey, ideals are social instruments. Ideals are plans or instruments for changing society for the better. All ideals must be examined in the light of their social context and understood as instruments for changing social reality. God, according to Dewey, "denotes the unity of all ideal ends arousing us to desire and actions."[38] For Dewey, this "unity" was projected onto the ideal ends by the imagination. The word God means, "the ideal ends that, at a given time and place, one acknowledges as having authority over his volition and emotion, the values to which one is supremely devoted, as far as these ends, through imagination take on unity."[39] Kaplan took this instrumental notion from Dewey, but he thought of the unity not as a projection of the human imagination but as an objective unity. Thus he posited "the identification of the Divine with those forces in nature and society that generate and support ideals."[40] Looked upon as an instrument, God functions in such a way as to change human society and human nature for the better. To do this, God functions within human personality. Kaplan says, "There is something divine in human personality, in that it is the instrument through which the creative life of the world effects the evolution of the human race."[41]

We can get some feel for the way in which Kaplan understands God as instrument if we look at the way in which he defines sovereignty. To speak of God as sovereign is to speak of "that Power on which we rely for the regeneration of society and which operates through individual human beings and social institutions."[42] God is the idea that changes society for the better. "Faith in the sovereignty of God comes then to mean faith that in mankind there is manifest a Power which, in full harmony with the nature of the physical universe, operates for the regeneration of human society."[43]

4.   Ahad Ha-Am

Another source for Kaplan's constructive position was the writings of Ahad Ha-Am, the pen name of Asher Ginzberg, which in Hebrew means "one of the People." Kaplan was slow in acknowledging his dependence on Ahad Ha-Am. In his magnum opus *Judaism as a Civilization*, written in 1934, Kaplan refers to Ahad Ha-Am only in passing and in a depreciating manner.[44] Not until 1942 in "The Influences That Have Shaped My Life" did Kaplan publicly acknowledge the influence of Ahad Ha Am.[45] Still later, in 1970, he dedicated *The Religion of Ethical Nationhood* to the memory of Ahad Ha-Am. Even though he did not credit his writings, some of the early statements of Kaplan are very similar to those of Ahad Ha-Am. For example, in *The Future of the American Jew* Kaplan says, "We are faithful to the Jewish religion, not because we have chosen it as the best of all religions, but because it is ours, the only religion we have, an inseparable part of our collective personality as a people."[46] The ideas expressed in this quotation are very similar to ideas found in the writings of Ahad Ha-Am. Ahad Ha-Am says about himself and other Jews that being a Jew is not so much a conscious decision as a natural sentiment arising out of membership in a group. He says,

> Nobody asked us before we were born, do you want to be Jews? Do you like the teachings of Judaism, the Torah of Judaism? Judaism introduced us into its covenant without our knowledge or consent and gave us a completed Torah that preceded our own creation....Why are we Jews? How strange the very question! ...It is within us; it is one of our laws of nature. It has an existence and a constancy of its own, like a mother's love for her children, like a man's love of his homeland.[47]

Ahad Ha-Am was more interested in the cultural aspects of Judaism than in its religious aspects, but his idea that the Jewish nation had a national will-to-live in accordance with prophetic ideals paralleled Kaplan's notion of religion as the collective consciousness of a people which sanctioned "the ideals and purposes of the group."[48]

For Ahad Ha-Am there is within the Jewish people a "national will to live."[49] This national will to live is not mere survival but a will to live in accordance with the principles of absolute justice first set forth by the prophets.[50] The Jew strives to live in accordance with the principles of absolute justice not primarily because the Jew as an individual makes a conscious decision to act justly but because the individual belongs to a nation whose collective personality or consciousness, to use Kaplan's term, is animated by spiritual values.[51]

Although it is obvious that there is a great similarity between Ahad Ha-Am's and Kaplan's notion of peoplehood or nationhood, Kaplan himself was slow in acknowledging this closeness. Aaron Lor in a dissertation, *Processes in Judaism: Ahad Ha-Am and Mordecai M. Kaplan*, puts forth the thesis that Kaplan did not fully appreciate the positive influence that Ahad Ha-Am had on him until long after he had incorporated some of the latter's basic ideas into his own writings. Lor quotes from "The Way I have Come" published in 1952 as the point at which Kaplan realized and publicly noted his dependence on Ahad Ha-Am.[52] Richard Libowitz suggests that Kaplan was aware of his dependence on Ahad Ha-Am at an earlier date. Libowitz quotes Kaplan's words from an undated source to show Kaplan's awareness of Ahad Ha-Am's influence on him. "Reconstructionism is not a new movement. It is actually Ahad Ha-Am's Spiritual Zionism spelled out into an ideology which renders it applicable to world Jewry instead of merely the State of Israel."[53] Libowitz also quotes from "The Influences That Have Shaped My Life" where Kaplan says, "the Zionist movement and particularly the Ahad Ha-Amist conception of the Jewish people as a living organism, animated by an irresist-

ible will to live, enabled me to find spiritual anchorage."[54] From the published
material it is difficult to say how aware Kaplan was of his dependence on
Ahad Ha-Am before the 1940s or several years after the publication of
Judaism as a Civilization, but in his later works he both uses ideas from
Ahad Ha-Am and acknowledges the source.

From the above material we can see how Kaplan's idea of peoplehood
or Judaism as a spiritual civilization has affinities with Ahad Ha-Am's notion
of cultural Zionism. For Ahad Ha-Am, even in diaspora the genius of the
Jewish people has found expression. He says, "The unfavorable conditions in
which we have lived since the Dispersion have naturally left their mark on
our literary work; but the Jewish genius has undergone no change in its
essential character and has never ceased to produce."[55]

Because he agreed with Ahad Ha-Am that the people is the bearer of
spiritual values, Kaplan also accepted Ahad Ha-Am's notion that there could
be differing concepts of God and religion among Jewish people without this
destroying their essential unity.[56] In *The Future of the American Jew*, Kaplan
speaks of Judaism as a religious civilization.

> As such, Judaism is the ensemble of the following organically
> interrelated elements of culture: a feeling of belonging to a his-
> toric and indivisible people, rootage in a common land, a continu-
> ing history, a living language and literature, and common mores,
> laws and arts, with religion as the integrating soul-giving factor of
> all those elements.[57]

The religion of a civilization expresses a people's commitment to self-fulfillment for each individual within the community. Thus the religious task of
Judaism "is so to reinterpret the religious values of our tradition that they
would create in us a passionate desire to strive unitedly as Jews for the
purpose of helping one another to become fully human."[58] Since religion is a
civilization's expression of what is best for human self-fulfillment, it follows

that people with different concepts and ideas can work together in order to provide a better life for every single person. Thus Kaplan can say "the Jewish religion can no longer be required to be entirely uniform in its beliefs and practices."[59]

In an earlier work, *The Meaning of God in Modern Jewish Religion*, he makes the same point.

> *The religious community is based not so much on common ideas as on common interests, common experiences, common hopes, fears and yearnings; it is a community of the heart rather than of the mind.*[60]

Because this is so, "its members can worship God in common, experience together the sense of His presence, even though they may have the most diverse conceptions of Him and of the nature of their communion with Him."[61] While agreeing with Ahad Ha-Am on the importance of peoplehood and on the plurality of religious views within Judaism, Kaplan differed with him on other no less significant points. Following Durkheim, Kaplan was convinced of the importance of ritual and worship in maintaining and further-ing a group's sense of values. Thus he was less than pleased with the lack of attention to religious practice manifested by Ahad Ha-Am.[62] For Kaplan, religious practices and public worship give us a sense of a supportive power that is at work in others and in each individual. "The presence of others participating with us in articulating our common ideals assures us that we are not separate drops of life, but parts of the mighty current of human life."[63] Furthermore, group worship takes a person out of self concern and helps such a one to identify with the cares and problems of others. "Participation in public worship breaks through the prison of the ego," so that, "instead of living but one small and petty life, we now share the multitudinous life of our people."[64] Worship also gives the individual a sense of immortality. As Kaplan says, "Through our worship as part of a religious community that outlives all its members, this sense of our life's triumph over death and all manner of frustration is brought home to us."[65]

Kaplan also saw his notion of Zionism as significantly different from Ahad Ha-Am, though both espoused a spiritual Zionism as opposed to a political Zionism. Ahad Ha-Am, as Kaplan understood him, saw the establishment of a community in Palestine as the beginning of a process of education that would revive a spirit of nationalism in diaspora Jews, the result of which would be that all Jews would migrate back to Israel and help in the Jewish renaissance going on there.[66] Kaplan, however, saw this as a practical impossibility.[67] Historically, according to Kaplan, even when threatened by the nations in which they lived, few diaspora Jews opted to go to Israel. Those now living in the United States where Jews are accepted and free to practice their religion are even less likely to want to return. What is needed is to stress the interdependence of the Jews in Israel and those in diaspora. Zionism

> should henceforth embrace as its objective not only the security and growth of the state of Israel but also the reaffirmation of the unity of the Jewish People throughout the world, redefinition of its group status, and the revitalization of the Jewish spiritual heritage as a bond to unite the scattered Jewish communities with one another and with the Jewish community in Israel[68]

Relation to Contemporary versions of Judaism

Kaplan's acceptance of the scientific world view as definitive of what was real made him turn to modern sociologists, pragmatists and secular Zionists for insights on how to rethink religious problems. In this section, we will look at Kaplan's relation to different schools of contemporary Judaism in order to show more clearly his relation to the American Empirical tradition and to highlight the distinctive elements in his own constructive position.

1.   Reform Judaism

Although there are some early congregations and movements in the United
States that can be called Reform, Reform Judaism as a continuing vibrant
movement can be dated from the advent of Isaac Meyer Wise on the American scene. He "designed and erected the three pillars upon which the Reform
edifice stands today: the Union of American Hebrew Congregations, the
Hebrew Union College and the Central Conference of American Rabbis."[69] For
Wise, the essence of Judaism consisted of moral principles; thus Judaism was
neither a system of beliefs, a form of worship, nor a set of observances. The
Ten Commandments were the primary source for ethical principles and these
ethical principles were what Wise meant by religion. These ethical principles
formed the kernel of Judaism; the shell, *i.e.*, the observances and beliefs,
could take different forms, but the kernel remained the same. Wise saw these
unchanging principles as forming the basis of a universal faith. Moreover, this
universal religion could be adapted to the contemporary American scene and
there was no need to conform to the historical practices and beliefs of an
earlier age.

Reform Judaism, with its emphasis on taking the modern world seriously and its insistence that laws and rituals can change with the changing
circumstances of life, would seem to be compatible with Kaplan's basic
outlook, and there are some similarities. Both Kaplan and Wise held that
beliefs, laws, and rituals could change without doing violence to that which
was essential in Judaism. Yet, they differed on what they saw as essential to
Judaism. Wise, following the program of the German Idealists, found the
essence of Judaism to lie in universal principles. Kaplan, on the other hand,

found the essence of Judaism to consist in a historical, living people. Wise and the Pittsburgh Conference understood Judaism as "a progressive religion, ever striving to be in accord with the postulates of reason."[70] In contrast, Kaplan understood Judaism as a religious civilization. Religious beliefs and practices did not change in accordance with the postulates of reason but in accordance with the needs of a vibrant community. Both Reform Judaism and Kaplan accept the notion of evolution, but Reform theologians were talking about the evolution of abstract ideas whereas Kaplan was concerned about the changes within Judaism that emerge out of the concrete historical situation. For Kaplan, ideas and moral values changed in accordance with the needs of a given cultural group or people. Moral values do evolve as a consequence of the interaction of humanity and God, but the tie to the empirical situation is more fundamental and important than the Reform theologians realize. Thus Kaplan charges that the Reform adherents substitute platitudinous morals for the living reality of Israel's Torah.[71] The ancient Torah was designed as a blue-print for a living nation. What is therefore required, if Judaism is to survive, is a revaluation of what the nation or Jewish people needs in order to heighten its group consciousness. The Torah needs to be associated once again with a group that is striving to do battle against present day evils and trying to provide a more satisfying and fulfilling life for its members.[72] Insofar as Reform Judaism, with its idealized universals, down-plays the importance of the Jewish people or nation, it actually cuts out of Judaism that which is necessary for its survival. With Durkheim, Kaplan espouses the necessary bond between a given culture and its religion. "The peoplehood, the culture, and the religion of the Jews are one and inseparable."[73] For Kaplan, then, a people's religion is part of its collective consciousness or personality. To do away with the distinctive group or to down-play its importance is finally to jeopardize the religion itself. Religion is not a collection of abstract ideals, but arises out of the concrete historical struggle of a people to provide a better and morally fulfilling life for its members. As Kaplan clearly puts the matter:

> The entire program of Reformism is based on a misconception of the very nature of a religion like that of the Jewish people. Such a religion never evolved apart from the people that evolved it, and cannot be treated as a system of ideas and practices which might be fostered by a religio-philosophical group. The religion of a people is but a phase of the entire life of that people and determined by the forces, social, economic and cultural, inherent in its life, as well as by the fortunes attending it.[74]

Kaplan rejects the approach of Reform Judaism, not only because it undermines the group consciousness of a people, but also because the abstract values and morals which form its basic principles are too ethereal to be adequate instruments of social change. Religion, if it is to survive, must not provide abstract principles but instruments or blueprints for changing a given society for the better.[75] This criticism of Reform Judaism comes from Kaplan's acceptance of Dewey's notion that truth is instrumental.[76] It also comes from his understanding of the role the Torah has played in the life of the Jewish people. The Torah arose from the living needs of an evolving civilization, not from the contemplation of philosophical truths. It also provided concrete guidance for a people as it moved from one historical context to another. Therefore, the Torah needs to be viewed dynamically, "as subject to change and development."[77] Kaplan likens the original Torah of the Pentateuch to the Constitution. It is the Bill of Rights which has kept the Constitution from becoming static and outmoded. In the same way, the interpretations of the tradition kept the Biblical Torah from becoming static and unrelated to life. The message for the modern Jew is that "whatever new developments take place in Jewish life, in democratic response to new and unprecedented challenges and urgencies, should be regarded as Torah and as equally binding."[78]

Kaplan's basic critique of Reform Judaism is that it fails to take seriously the concrete historical situation in its formulation of truth. Like his mentors, James and Dewey, he does not look for truth outside of the experienced situation but sees truth as that which "gives us the fullest and most just expression of human interests while permitting us to survive in specific environments."[79] Ideas are not true because they correspond to some essential realm. Ideas, especially moral ideas, are true if they are workable. A moral idea is true or workable "if it leads to a higher level of enduring *satisfaction* of a wide range of human interests for the total community in the context of a given environment."[80] For Kaplan, as for James and Dewey, moral truth is related to our ability to anticipate the consequences of our actions. To a certain extent truth is created, because it is only after we have made a commitment or started on a course of action and seen the results of our actions that a certain course be called true. Truth remains in the realm of possibility until it is proved to work, *i.e.*, make life better for those within a certain group, in a certain place, in a certain time. Truth is immanent, part of the historical situation, not something that stands apart from the world.[81]

2.   Neo-Orthodox Judaism

Neo-Orthodoxy is another contemporary movement within Judaism that Kaplan criticizes as not being a viable alternative for the Jew who accepts a modern world-view. For Kaplan, Neo-Orthodoxy was represented by such figures as Solomon Rapoport, Samuel David Luzzatto, Nathan Marcus Adler, and

Samson Raphael Hirsch. For Kaplan, these adherents of Neo-Orthodoxy differ
from traditional Judaism or Orthodoxy in three fundamental respects.

In the first place, the older Orthodoxy lived withdrawn from and
uninterested in the currents of thought of the modern world.[82] The Neo-Orthodox, although attempting to follow all the ritualistic rules and practices of the
tradition, do so in the face of changing circumstances, historical studies, and
the findings of modern science. The Neo-Orthodox are conscious of the way
in which their understanding contradicts the findings of modern historical and
evolutionary science in a way in which the Orthodox were not.[83] The older
Orthodox communities could practice their religion and live in accordance
with traditional practice because the total community life was structured by
the tradition. With the coming of emancipation and the entering of the Jew
into the full life of the nation, however, there are practical difficulties that
arise. How can a religious Jew take time off for all the holidays and still
retain his job in a culture where few of the other workers need or want to
have that time off? To the question, "are the ceremonial laws binding in a
setting that makes them very difficult to observe?" the Neo-Orthodox answers,
"yes." God's plan for the Jewish people is unchanging and thus, regardless of
the changing conditions of life, Jews are bound to follow the rules and
regulations laid down.[84]

In the second place, Kaplan notes that the Neo-Orthodox differ from
their traditional interpreters in their understanding of election or the meaning
of Israel as a nation. According to Kaplan, "the traditional belief as formulated by Judah Ha-Levi is that Israel was privileged to come into the possession of the Torah on account of the inherent superiority which it had inherited
from Adam, Noah and the Patriarchs, and which marked it off as a higher
human species."[85] The Neo-Orthodox re-interpret that belief and maintain "it is
for the sake of the Torah, for the sake of preserving and propagating the

teachings of that Torah, and not because of any hereditary superiority, that God chose Israel."[86] For the older Orthodoxy, the nation of Israel was inherently superior to the nations around them. For the New Orthodoxy there is nothing inherently superior about Israel except that it is the vehicle for giving the Torah to the world.[87]

In the third place, the Neo-Orthodox differ from the Orthodox in their valuation of the Diaspora. For the older Orthodoxy, diaspora living was always an unqualified evil, a source of sorrow, something that was to be regretted. The hope of the Orthodox was always to return to the land. For the newer group, the very fact that the land is no more means that they can concentrate on living the life according to the Torah without the distraction and concerns involved in living within a sovereign nation. For the Neo-Orthodox, power is only temporary but life lived in accordance with the Torah is eternally satisfying. Further, all that the Jews have had to suffer in order to maintain life in accordance with Torah—despite their exile—has made of them a nation of true heroes. Finally, under the conditions of emancipation, the Jews are free "to live the Israel-life in all its grandeur."[88]

Kaplan's chief criticism of the Neo-Orthodox is that they have made the Torah binding and yet have eliminated from the Torah all of the civil law; only the ritual law needs to be observed. In doing this the Neo-Orthodox have cut Torah off from the everyday existence of the people; the law no longer deals with the way in which a people should live; Judaism becomes not a nation but a ritual community. Civil law, which directs the everyday life of a group, becomes non-existent. For Kaplan, ritual cannot endure if it is not essentially related to the total social and civil structure of a group. To cut off the civil law from ritual law is to deny the reality of the group which ritual should be celebrating.[89] Only by re-interpreting the Torah so that it functions as a way of life for a people can the ritual practices endure. The Durkheimian understanding of the relation of ritual to group life is obviously the underlying notion in Kaplan's critique.

Kaplan's criticism of Neo-Orthodoxy is similar to his criticism of Reform Judaism. For Kaplan, both Neo-Orthodoxy and Reform Judaism fail to take seriously that religion arises out of the historical experiences of a people. In "Judaism as a Civilization," which appeared in the *S. A. J. Review*, Kaplan speaks of the experience which constitutes the Jewish heritage in the following manner,

> We regard the heritage neither as a static system of beliefs and practices, nor as a religious philosophy of life with a number of corollaries for human conduct, nor as a supernaturally revealed complex of laws, but as the social and psychological momentum of the life of a nation known as the Jewish people, with the laws of self-development and self-perpetuation that are common to the lives of all nations, and constituting, for the purposes of criticism and incorporation into a program, a complex of language, folkways, patterns of social habits, and standards of conduct and spiritual ideals.[90]

Neo-Orthodoxy takes a pattern (the ritual law) from an assumed supernatural realm and applies it to a given situation without regard for historical changes. Reform talks about universal ethical principles that it then seeks to apply to concrete situations without realizing that ethical principles must arise out of the interactions of individuals within a given community.[91] Neither the Orthodox nor the Reform see truth as arising out of the needs of a living community.[92] As Kaplan sees it, the ritual law of the Neo-Orthodox is no longer an expression of a living dynamic community. It belongs to a realm that has no real contact with the world in which the contemporary Jew must live. It is a romantic fossil that makes living in the present even more difficult. Furthermore, because it begins with a Torah that is totally unrelated to the needs and understandings of modern people, Neo-Orthodoxy provides no program of action by which it can effectively teach the Torah to non-Jews, even though one of its explicit purposes is to propagate the teachings of Torah to the world.[93] From Kaplan's perspective, the watered down Torah of the Neo-Orthodox neither represents the spiritual life of contemporary Jewish people nor does it offer a way of living to those outside Judaism.

3.   Conservative Judaism

It would seem that Kaplan, who has a deep concern for the unity of the Jewish people and an interest in the scientific study of Jewish history, would find Conservative Judaism congenial. Kaplan, however, criticized Conservativism as harshly as Reform and Neo-Orthodoxy. At the time in which he wrote *Judaism as a Civilization*, Kaplan could find no systematic presentation of Conservativism. He therefore had to draw on his own experiences with his teachers and colleagues at Jewish Theological Seminary and on occasional statements in their published writings.[94] Before presenting his criticism of the movement, however, it is important to give a short sketch of the history and basic ideas of Conservative Judaism.

Moshe Davis, in The *Emergence of Conservative Judaism*, has given us a good background and history of the early days of the movement while Herbert Parzen, in *Architects of Conservative Judaism*, has provided us with an account of the founding and continuing history of The Jewish Theological Seminary, including a chapter on Kaplan.[95] According to Davis, Conservative Judaism grew out of the 19th century "Historical School." In Europe this Historical School could boast of such thinkers as Nachman Krochmal, Leopold Zuna, Solomon Rapoport, and Zacharias Frankel. This school stressed that the "divine character of the Jewish Law, taught by the Orthodox,"[96] and "the moral purpose stressed by Reform"[97] had to be understood in light of the totality of Jewish experience. By focusing on the totality of Jewish experience throughout the ages it was possible for those with very different interpretations of Judaism to be included under its banner. Thus, when The Jewish Theological Seminary came into existence, it could boast of the support of synagogues that were very Orthodox and of the support of synagogues that had decided Reform leanings.[98] Both Dr. Sabato Morais and Dr. H. Pereira Mendes, the first two heads of the Seminary, were inclined toward Orthodoxy and seminary education under their administration tended to maintain the immutability of revelation as Mordecai Kaplan has attested.[99] Solomon Schecter, a disciple of Zacharias Frankel, became head of the Seminary in 1902. He held to the divine origin of the Torah, but at the same time held that "Catholic Israel" or the people as a whole have a right to determine what will continue to be the practices of the community.[100] He was much more interested in maintaining the importance of the history of the Jewish people and thus could tolerate different understandings of revelation and of the Jewish law.[101]

This diverse background may account for Kaplan's main criticism of Conservative Judaism; that Conservativism is so unsure as to what its basic principles are that it can provide no viable plan that will allow for facing the new conditions and needs of the Jewish people.[102] A related criticism is that Conservativism emphasizes observances and ceremonies, but it fails to provide a rationale for why these are important for the life of the community. It cannot say with Neo-Orthodoxy that these observances are necessary because they were given by God at Sinai, because Conservative Judaism also emphasizes the importance of reason. Kaplan points out that "reason" in the modern, naturalistic context necessarily rejects revelation. Indeed Conservatives say that when the consensus of the community regards a given observance as no longer valid, it can be eliminated. Thus many of the Biblical laws are obsolete in our day and age. Even with regard to what is meant by revelation, the Conservative position is ambiguous. Revelation can mean the mystery that happened at Sinai or it can refer to "a more sensitive conscience, a greater ability to distinguish between right and wrong."[103] As Kaplan sees it, Conservative Judaism tries to maintain a distinction between the eternal truths and the historical form in which they appear, but it provides no criteria for distinguishing what the eternal essence is and what the historical conditioning is.[104] For Kaplan, who sees truth as emerging out of the conditions of life of a given people, this attempt to separate essence from concrete existence makes no sense. His insistence that values and principles, and the laws that embody them, grow out of the historical experiences of a people keep him from supporting a Conservativism that attempts to separate essence and existence.

Relation to the American Empirical Movement

From the above criticisms of what he sees as dominant trends within the Jewish tradition, we can see that Kaplan is clearly within what I have called the American Empirical Tradition in theology: theology that draws on socio-historical and relational data as primary sources and that sees value and meaning as arising out of the concrete experienced situation. The person within this tradition with whom Kaplan has the most in common theologically is Henry Nelson Wieman. Interestingly enough, there does not seem to have been any collaboration between them as they developed their understandings about the source of values and their ideas about God, yet the terminologies they use and their conceptions of God are amazingly similar. They both speak of God in terms of process, power, and creativity, and they both assume that

God is that aspect of the universe that promotes human good. Both men recognized the close parallels in their thought in articles written to celebrate Kaplan's 70th birthday. Kaplan wrote at that time, "I am grateful to Prof. Wieman for having taken the trouble to set forth his own conception of God. His statements prove how remarkably parallel, though independently, our lines of thinking have run."[105] Wieman agreed on the parallel nature of their thought in the following words: "I have given my version of the idea of God which I think is basically in accord with Dr. Kaplan's."[106]

Both Kaplan and Wieman speak of God as function and not as person. In *The Source of Human Good,* Wieman speaks of God as creative event, and denies both the traditional doctrine of transcendence and the personal character of God. "The creative event is the actual reality doing the work in history which has been mythically attributed to a transcendental person, even though the real source of human good is neither transcendental nor a person."[107] In speaking of God as function, they mean that there is a process in the universe that is at work to bring about a more fulfilling life for humanity. In *The Future of The American Jew,* Kaplan says,

> We suggest that God be thought of as the cosmic process that makes for man's life abundant or salvation. As cosmic process, God is more than a physical, chemical, biological, psychological, or even social process. God includes them all, but what is distinctive about the God-process is that it is superfactual and superexperiential.[108]

He goes on to say, "Thinking of God as process rather than as entity in no way tends to make Him less real."[109] Indeed for both Kaplan and Wieman being able to identify God as a process makes God more real and more experienceable. In *The Source of Human Good,* these words appear:

> Creativity is not beyond all human appreciation. It can be appreciated, and, when proper social conditions and required

knowledge have been achieved, it can be known as a part of the temporal, spatial, material world.[110]

At the end of this same volume he adds, "God, according to this interpretation, is immediately accessible to human living and human feeling in all the fullness of his concrete reality."[111] Humanity's role then is to discover the process that produces a higher level of human fulfillment and to increase the conditions that facilitate the process's action or, to use Wieman's terms, increase the conditions that promote qualitative meaning.

Both Kaplan and Wieman view religion as rooted in the lived experience of a group, but whereas Kaplan stresses the people, the distinct ethnic group, as the central reality for his theologizing, Wieman wants to stress that which is most real to all human beings within whatever religious tradition they find themselves. Wieman is more clearly a philosopher of religion while Kaplan, in so far as he is interpreting or reinterpreting a specific religious tradition to which he is committed, is more clearly a theologian. Wieman "wishes to stress that the empirical approach to the study of God is available to all men everywhere and that its results are to be affirmed not only confessionally but with all the objectivity that attaches to the conclusions of any empirical investigation."[112] Thus, while Kaplan tends to stress those God-functions that make it possible for a given religious civilization to survive, Wieman, though not discounting the particular religious community, tends to focus on those aspects of God's function that are available to all persons of inquiring mind. The practical result has been that Kaplan has influenced Judaism and the Jewish religion to a far greater extent than Wieman has influenced Christianity.

Wieman says, and he thinks that Kaplan is in substantial agreement with him, that all power is related to process, and every power is a process. As he says,

> Power is process; process is power. Examine any instance of power, such as the explosion of an atomic bomb, or a leader inspiring many men to heroic struggle and utmost effort. What do you find? You always find a process of transformation and nothing else.[113]

Thus for him to look for those things in the world that promote human good means that he is looking for a definite process or power. By putting the matter in these terms, Wieman thinks he has overcome the criticism that process implies a plurality of events whereas power stresses a unifying agent.

His way of addressing the issue, however, really does not solve the problem. One is still left with either a unity that is merely an abstraction, the kind of unity that says all things that promote good equal God, or one is left saying that God is that power which causes individual goods and thus one has overstepped the empirical evidence. More time will be spent with this problem when we are considering Kaplan's constructive position. Suffice it to say here that both men begin with Dewey's notion of God as a function of human reason and both men run into trouble when they try to make that function of the mind into an objective datum in the world. For Dewey, God was a term used for the synthesizing of values and has subjective validity only. When one tries to make the term stand for an objective synthesis of values that is described as both process and power, one is left with the logical problems noted above.

Kaplan's Constructive Position

1.   Major Concern

The major concern that is manifest throughout Mordecai Kaplan's writings is for the survival and revitalization of the Jewish people as a vibrant and active participant within the modern world. He sought to provide a rationale and a program for the continuation of the Jewish people as a living ethnic-cultural entity. He insisted that any group, whatever its basis, had a right to survive as long as it was not antagonistic to other groups or to the larger nation in which it found itself.[114] His concern is for Judaism to do more than survive, however. He wanted to provide a rationale and a master plan for Judaism that would assure Judaism would continue to be a changing, modern community. His basic rationale is incorporated in his major work, *Judaism as a Civilization*. As Kaplan saw it, the traditional reasons for assuming that the Jewish people should continue were no longer valid given the modern age within which we live. He saw the need to reinterpret the meaning of the Jewish tradition so that the Jewish Civilization could maintain itself as a living organic unity within the modern age without cutting itself off from its traditional past.[115] This "need" is the basis of Kaplan's program of revaluation or reinterpretation of the tradition.

In *The Religion of Ethical Nationhood*, Kaplan speaks of the dilemma that faced him when he saw the basic contradictions between his Jewish tradition and the modern world view. Kaplan quotes Suzanne E. Langer, author of *Philosophy in a New Key*:

> I left religion during college... When I began to have faith in my mind and my feeling of insecurity disappeared, religion became untenable and therefore dispensable.[116]

Yet, Kaplan, on the other hand, found the impact of modern thought, while forcing him to seek ways of rethinking traditional beliefs and practices, did not make him reject the values of traditional religion.

> Although my own experience as a young Orthodox rabbi was similar, my conclusion was different. While ministering to my congregation, I began to have more faith in my own mind than in the Orthodox Jewish tradition in which I had been educated. But I decided to leave the Orthodox rabbinate, not Judaism. Following the dictates of reason, I conceived of Judaism as the evolving religious civilization of the Jewish people. And ever since I have sought ideological validation of the Jewish people's will to resume its historic role as a "light to the nations."[117]

Instead of rejecting Judaism and the Jewish people, Kaplan attempted an apologetic, a reasoned defense of the validity of Judaism and the Jewish religion within a modern framework. This task of reinterpretation is a religious task. It is an attempt to preserve Judaism as a religious civilization and to make belonging to that civilization a viable option for the Jew perplexed by the conflict between the modern world view and the traditional understanding of the nation as elected by a supernatural God. His reinterpretation is for those Jews who have a reverence and feeling for the values and community life of Judaism but who are no longer at home within any of the current religious denominations within Judaism. Whereas Maimonides was said to have only one perplexed Jew who needed a reconstructed Judaism, Kaplan notes that the number of such Jews today is legion. "Why not offer them some plausible version of Judaism?"[118]

Kaplan argues that the concept of otherworldliness that was one of the greatest influences in keeping the traditional Jewish people together is no longer possible given the modern world view.[119] He argues that there is one thing that will keep the Jewish people unified even in the modern world—and that is the realization that Jewish civilization is of value in and of itself. Kaplan continues:

> Although the primary cohesive force which held the Jewish people together—the traditional conception of other-worldly salvation—has practically become inoperative, there has developed in the course of the centuries of living, thinking and suffering together a *secondary* cohesive force which manifests itself in the will to maintain and perpetuate Jewish life as something desirable in and for itself.[120]

Unlike the traditional Jews who assumed that Judaism as a people and a religion would endure because the nation was the special elect of God, the modern Jew is forced to face the possibility that Judaism both as a people and as a religion will dissolve. The Jews, in order to survive, must intentionally plan for their continuance because there is no supernatural force that will guarantee their survival as a people. "Jews must focus their mind and heart upon the task of giving purpose and direction to what is at present little more than a blind urge to live as Jews."[121] The whole of Kaplan's career as an author, teacher, and social planner is concerned with providing a rationale for this "blind urge," this gut feeling that the Jewish people are of intrinsic worth, regardless of the historical change that has taken place which might make it difficult to recognize the twentieth century Jew as belonging to the same people as did Maimonides or the Maccabeans.

2.   Scientific World View

Since Kaplan's program is to reconcile Judaism with the modern world, it is important to understand how he views the modern world and scientific world view. When speaking about science and natural law theory Kaplan tends to speak of them as normative rather than descriptive. Here I want to employ what Thomas S. Kuhn means by that distinction in *The Structure of Scientific Revolutions*. A normative understanding means that natural laws are somehow given in the structure of the universe and thus cannot be challenged. Natural laws, understood as descriptions, however, mean that so far as has been observed within a certain area or field of observation, a certain paradigm seems to be applicable. In other words, scientific "laws" arise from theories that represent the general consensus as to what are the important problems and the best way at the moment to deal with them, given the current state of observation. It is because Kaplan understands natural laws as normative that he can make the following statement in an unqualified manner:

> The fact that the nature of God is beyond our understanding does not mean that we can afford to conceive of Him in terms that are clearly not true in accordance with the highest standards of truth. Our conception of God must be self-consistent and consistent with whatever else we hold to be true.[122]

What Kaplan holds to be true are natural laws that apply to God as well as to scientific data. He believes in uniformities in the cosmos that are expressed in natural laws. Thus he argues, "We cannot, for example, believe that God performs miracles, and at the same time believe in the uniformities of natural law demanded by scientific theory."[123] If Kuhn is right, of course, science does not need to believe in such uniformities of natural law in order to carry out its business. All it needs is to believe that a given hypothesis is sufficiently broad to take in a given amount of data. The point is, however, that Kaplan thinks that science has the final say about what is or is not possible in the religious realm as well as in all other realms of life. Religion must conform to the dictates of scientific reason.

3. Revaluation

Revaluation is the word Kaplan uses to describe the attempt to take traditional ideas and translate them into notions that make sense within a modern scientific age without doing violence to the basic value of human fulfillment found in the ancient idea.[124] For revaluation to be successful, it will not only

> treat the Torah, which is the core of Jewish social heritage, as a human product and therefore as reflecting the limitations of the various periods during which its contents were formulated, but, moreover, it will have to discover to what extent the values of the Jewish social heritage have made for the complete development of the individual and the unification of society."[125]

While asserting that each age has reinterpreted the God-idea and changed its religious practices in order to accommodate the needs of people in different ages, Kaplan sees a difference between what he is doing and what was done by reinterpreters within the Jewish tradition prior to the modern age. In the past, the traditional reinterpreters of Judaism were largely unconscious about what they were doing. "Before historic research or before any of the social sciences were born, men lacked the historic perspective which might have made them aware of the discrepancy between the original meaning of a sacred text or a ritual practice and their understanding of it."[126] Because they were unaware of historical conditioning, they assumed that their ideas and understandings were the same as that of the original authors.[127] Thus they had no problem with reading their own ideas, beliefs, and needs into the traditional material.

Kaplan calls the method used by the ancients "transvaluation." For him, transvaluation "consists in ascribing meanings to the traditional content of a religion or social heritage, which could neither have been contemplated nor implied by the authors of that content."[128] The way in which the meaning of a scriptural text changes in the tradition is apparent in an example Kaplan gives from the book of Exodus, Exodus 20:21.[129] There the original text clearly says that God will bless the sacrifices of the people in every place where they offer them to God. During the second Commonwealth, the text was interpreted to mean that sacrifices would be acceptable only in one place.[130] Another text in Exodus (Ex. 21:24) limits the vengeance that can be exacted by establishing an eye for an eye, a tooth for a tooth. The rabbis who wished to maintain the authoritative character of scripture, and at the same time bound by a different set of moral standards, interpret this text as referring to monetary compensation.[131] Again, this was not a conscious reading back into the text, but simply the assumption that the moral standards current in their day must be the same as the standards that prevailed in ancient times. The allegorists from Philo onward were also part of this tradition of transvaluation. They are part of it because they held that the original text held the allegorical as well as the literal meaning from the beginning.

Transvaluation is no longer a possibility for the modern Jew. Only ignorance of historical and social changes makes transvaluation possible. Our age in which evolution and change are understood as part of the historical process requires another solution. The solution Kaplan proposes is "revaluation." "Revaluation consists in disengaging from the traditional content those elements in it which answer permanent postulates of human nature, and in integrating them into our ideology."[132] What Kaplan means may be clearer for us if we recall the relation of "needs," "goods,"[133] and "values" that is set forth in the works of John Dewey. According to Dewey both needs and values are social terms. Needs are such things as the need to feel secure, the need to be in a friendly environment, the psychological need an individual has to fulfill self-potential within a particular situation.[134] We might add here the need to make sense of all aspects of the world within whatever world view is current for the individual. Fulfillment of those needs for an individual is a good but it is not a value if the fulfillment of those needs denies to someone else the possibility of attaining like fulfillment.[135] This is clear in Dewey's discussion of democracy.

> All social institutions have a meaning, a purpose. That purpose is to set free and develop the capacities of human individuals without respect to race, sex, class or economic status. And this is all one with saying that the test of their value is the extent to which they educate every individual into the full stature of his possibility. Democracy has many meanings, but if it has a moral meaning, it is found in resolving that the supreme test of all political institutions and industrial arrangements shall be the contribution they make to the all-around growth of every member of society.[136]

That is why, from Dewey's point of view, totalitarianism is wrong even if great art or things of beauty are commissioned and created. Value implies that all people within a culture can benefit. Needs, according to Dewey, arise out of the concrete situation. Values are correlative to these needs, but values are never simply individualistic, but are correlative to social or group needs. Values are created when the intellect focuses on the needs and tries to find new or better ways to fulfill these needs. In an essay, entitled "The Construction of Good," which appeared as part of the Gifford lectures of 1929, Dewey says,

> What is needed is intelligent examination of the consequences that are actually effected by inherited institutions and customs, in order that there may be intelligent consideration of the ways in which they are to be intentionally modified in behalf of generation of different consequences."[137]

In other words, values can be arrived at in the same way as results are arrived at in a scientific experiment. For Dewey, in the past, "values" may

have been arrived at haphazardly without conscious realization of how value
came into being.

The introduction of the scientific method made a difference, and not
just in relation to material changes. Now it is possible to look at society,
come to an understanding of what the needs are for the members of that
society, form a hypothesis about how best to go about fulfilling those needs,
and test out how well that hypothesis works in meeting those needs. If it is
workable, not just for isolated individuals, or for an elite group within society,
but for all members within a society, then the hypothesis attains the status of
a value. "Values" are those things that help individuals fulfill their needs
within a given social context. Values direct conduct, they are instruments for
action which grow out of basic needs within a given society or institution.[138]

Kaplan tries to get at that which is constant in the ancient and the
modern world view. To get at that which is constant he makes use of
Dewey's analysis of the relation between needs and values. Dewey suggests
that there are basic needs which people have and that in each age these basic
needs ought to find fulfillment.[139] Kaplan made use of this relation between
needs and values, for example, in his discussion of worship. One of humanity's basic needs is to have reverence for or worship for that in the universe
which aids in the search for the most fulfilling life.[140] In a premodern age or
prescientific age, one can consider it a value to worship only the one God
and to denounce idolatry. In a scientific age a person can consider worship a
value, not when it is directed towards a supernatural God, but when it is
directed to "whatever in human nature or in the world about him enhances
human life."[141] The ancients thought that a supernatural God was interested in
their welfare. For them, God had created the world and the world to come.[142]
The modernist tries to see in the natural world, processes that can be of
benefit. As Kaplan says, "We have to identify as godhead, or as the divine

quality of universal being, all the relationships, tendencies and agencies which in their totality go to make human life worthwhile in the deepest and most abiding sense."[143] The common denominator for both ancient and modern individuals, as Kaplan sees it, is the concern for human fulfillment.

a.   The People

In his magnum opus, *Judaism as a Civilization*, Kaplan sought to revalue or re-interpret the significance of the Jewish community. In olden days the community was important because it guaranteed the individual's salvation conceived in otherworldly terms. Kaplan begins with the thesis that Judaism has always been influenced in its understanding of itself by outside forces. Thus in a day and age when the following propositions were accepted by the wider society, they tended to reinforce what the Jew also believed.

> 1. The Old Testament account of the creation of the world and of the beginnings of the human race is not only authentic, but constitutes the premise of all that men should believe in and strive for.

> 2. Human life on this earth, being full of sin and travail and ending in death, can attain its fulfillment or achieve salvation only in that perfect world which is known as the world to come.

> 3. The only way man can attain such salvation is by conducting himself in accordance with the supernaturally revealed will of God.[144]

Kaplan argues that since salvation was conceived of in other-worldly terms by the larger society, the Jewish community was influenced by those notions and accepted the then-current other-worldly conception. As long as the Jew believed that the law was handed down by supernatural forces at Sinai the Jew must believe that salvation, the attainment of life in the other world, is only possible through keeping that law.[145] Furthermore since the Jewish people were the only ones who had law or Torah which guaranteed salvation, the individual Jew had a great incentive for remaining within the Jewish community. "The only way in which the Jew believed it was possible for him to achieve salvation was by remaining loyal to his people, for it was only by sharing their life in this world that he was certain to share their life in the next world."[146] In a day and age when other-worldly notions are not widely accepted—indeed when the prevailing intellectual climate based on naturalistic science rejects the possibility of a life beyond this present one—there needs to be another interpretation of salvation, if the Jewish religion and the Jewish people are to continue.

In Kaplan's system salvation becomes the achievement of individual personality or self-fulfillment. The achievement of self-fulfillment is not possible, however, without interaction with a particular group to which the individual belongs. "This implies that one's people will always constitute one's chief source of salvation, and therefore one's chief medium of religion."[147] Kaplan develops both the symbol of the Sabbath and the concept of covenant in relation to this idea that salvation or human self-fulfillment is only possible within one's own group or civilization. The basic meaning of the Sabbath for the modern Jew is that on that day the Jew experiences "a renewed faith in the creative possibilities of life."[148] Along with this renewed faith comes the awareness that individual personality is enhanced by membership in the Jewish people.

> No individual is spiritually self-sufficient. The meanings and values that life has for him are a result of his relationship to the civilization in which he participates. The more that civilization

functions as a way of salvation, the more intense will be the individual's sense of identification with it.[149]

The Sabbath represents, then, the fact that the resources for a fulfilling life that individual Jews feel within their own person are mediated by the particular civilization of which they are a part.

The idea of covenant is another symbol that can be interpreted as stressing the importance of the continuing existence of the Jewish people for an individual's salvation. The notion of covenant means that a Jew is an inheritor of resources from the past that make it possible for the individual Jew to achieve personal fulfillment. Furthermore the notion of covenant means that the individual Jew is under obligation to pass those resources on to future descendants. Each national group or civilization has brought into the world certain experiences and values that help to make up the rich variety of the world. These values should be preserved but they cannot be preserved by anyone who is not intimately connected with that group. This lays a burden on the members of each group to do what they can to preserve the values and experiences of its own tradition.

> This is the answer to those who object to any specific commitments by reason of their being Jews. Such commitments are inherent in the very structure of society and civilization. Mankind is not all of one piece and, in the task of preserving and developing the spiritual heritage of the human race, the various historic groups have to assume responsibility, each one for the maintenance of its own identity as a contributor to the sum of human knowledge and experience.[150]

It is not possible to conceive of either individual salvation apart from a group or to think of salvation as being part of a world community. This is so because, "the basis of individuality and character is supplied not by the world at large with its multitudinous culture, but by the section of mankind which constitutes one's particular folk."[151] Folk religion, the religion of one's group, is absolutely essential for personal salvation. Kaplan describes folk religion as "the complex of habits and values by means of which the group life which a person shares becomes so significant to him as to constitute his self-fulfillment or at least the road to self-fulfillment."[152]

Of course, it follows from this that for a folk religion to continue it must demand the loyalty of its members and perpetuate its values through its members. "If the Jewish civilization is to evoke individual potentialities and to enrich the world of values, it must have folk religion."[153] Jewish Civilization must have a religion that expresses the soul or the essential character of the group that evolved it. Kaplan concludes with a statement that reveals his basic Durkheimian orientation.

> The outstanding generalization which emerges from the history of Judaism, and from its present struggle to continue, is that all spiritual values, from those of godhead to those of individual salvation are irrelevant and mischievous unless they are based upon the interests of some particular community, and unless they are applied to the life conditions there prevalent. The daily life and activity of a people should constitute the main source of its spiritual values. Unless those activities are transfigured and woven into a pattern of religious values, they leave the human spirit dwarfed, and likewise, unless religion is a product of vital activity, it dries up into an anarchism.[154]

Kaplan concludes with the seeming paradox that if the Jewish people are to have a spiritual renewal it is of the utmost importance that religion cease to be its sole preoccupation. Judaism can only survive if it continues to think of itself as a nation or people. Nationhood is not predicated on possession of power, but on the desire of a group to provide a worthwhile existence for its members. "A nation is not a fighting unit but a cultural group, united not by the instincts that keep together wolf-packs for purposes of offense and defense, but by the urge to develop differentias and potentialities which only collective life can bring forth."[155] In "Can Zionism Reconstitute the Jewish People?" Kaplan declares that the Jewish people are not a nation built on power, but "a religio-cultural, or Torah, people."[156]

b.   The Land

If the Jewish people are to continue as an organic whole, Kaplan sees the necessity for there to be a State of Israel. "There is nothing in traditional Judaism to suggest what Israel could do in the world as a landless people."[157] Although Reform Judaism saw no need for a Jewish land, Kaplan held that his revalued Judaism had to take account of the notion of the "land." He argued that "the function of nationhood can be discharged only through association with a definite territory, as the principal theatre of a people's collective life."[158] This state, as Kaplan envisioned it in 1948, could be part of a larger and more comprehensive body, even part of an Arab Federation.[159] All the Jews required was a territory in which they could continue to practice their religious civilization.

> Without Eretz Yisrael, Jewish culture tends to be limited to the confines of a Jewish cult, or to archaeological scholarship. With Eretz Yisrael, Judaism becomes a great historic movement with a present and a future as well as a past.[160]

This state is needed so that Jews throughout the world will have a focal point to look upon as they continue to maintain their ties to their Jewish civilization. Obviously, as Kaplan envisioned the state of Israel, it was not a nation built on power but on cultural and religious interests.[161] Therefore, he could suggest that the responsibility for military defense and foreign policy could be largely controlled by some other nation or international body, the British Empire, or the United Nations, for example.[162]

Jewish civilization in the diaspora needs the state of Israel and the state of Israel needs the Jewish civilization that flourishes in diaspora.

> Without Eretz Yisrael, there would be no motive for reconstructing Jewish life anywhere. Jewish life would lack that basic content which only Eretz Yisrael can supply—a living history which only the struggle to take root in a land can create, a collective consciousness which only a living language can beget, and common folkways which only the sharing of common practical concerns can evolve. But without a planned program of reconstruction of Jewish life in the Diaspora, Eretz Yisrael will lack the stimulus to recreate the elements of religion, law and education in the Jewish civilization.[163]

As we noted earlier, Kaplan is vitally concerned with preserving and continuing the life of this particular ethnic community. His concern for that community has lead him to see the necessity of having a particular area of land in which Jewish culture and religion can thrive. For him the best place is that bit of land where the Jewish people and their religion had their beginnings.[164] The community in Israel will act as a focus for the worldwide Jewish community. The Jewish community cannot survive, however, on the basis of its past. It must continue to adapt and change creatively with the times, which requires rethinking both the meaning of its common life and the values that have emerged and which continue to emerge. Only if the community in Israel continues to live creatively in the world can it then serve as a focus for Jews throughout the world. Jews in the diaspora need to maintain pressure on those in the State of Israel to maintain their religious task.[165] It is in *The Religion of Ethical Nationhood* that Kaplan most clearly sets forward a program for establishing a worldwide nation, a nation with its focus in Israel and linked to all the Jews in the diaspora. The kind of nation he visualizes is not a nation built on power, but one that practices cooperation with other nations and lives up to the highest of moral principles.

The nucleus for Jewish survival in the diaspora would be a Jewish Community Organization in each individual community. This organization would have six main functions. The first would be administrative. All Jews in a community would have to register and pay nominal dues. Doing these things would allow them the privilege of participating in communal elections, having a Jewish wedding, and being buried according to Jewish rites. Part of the administrative function would also be to raise funds for community uses such as the education of rabbis, the training of social workers, and institutional executives. In addition, there should be a department of statistics set up, (this obviously reflects Kaplan's bias as to the importance of sociology) to keep track of births, deaths, marriages, and other data of vital interest for the survival of the Jewish people. The second function of the Jewish Community Organization would be economic. It would help to soften the discrimination which Jews experience today in the various nations where they live. The third function would be the fostering of cultural life in the community. Besides establishing educational institutions for children and adults, the Jewish Community Organization would encourage literary and artistic creativity and provide for public worship and other forms of religious activity. The fourth function would be social service; taking care of all dependent classes such as the aged, orphaned, and refugees both at home and elsewhere in the world should have a high priority. The fifth function is what Kaplan calls Public Relations. Here Kaplan calls for the Jewish people's support of the state of Israel. Only through this active support will the Jewish people in the diaspora gain the sense of a spiritual focus and thus regain their dignity as a people. The sixth function is political. Kaplan envisions the Jews in local areas electing representatives to sit in a national body; this body would then have political clout when it speaks out on moral issues and Jewish rights.[166]

We cannot underestimate the importance of community structure for Kaplan. As he sees it, religion grows out of the needs and values of a people. "Group religion in all its forms represents man's groping efforts to achieve that dynamic equilibrium in the satisfaction of his needs which enables him to attain even higher levels of existence."[167] If the Jewish religion is going to flourish, then the organic community of which the Jew is a member must be sustained and continued. "You cannot have an authentic idea of God unless you belong to an organic community."[168] It is only in an organic community that the Jew can gain a sense of responsibility. It is this sense of responsibility as a member of a group that makes it possible for an individual to articulate personal ideas of God and human experience. Kaplan's notion of the idea of God as growing out of the experience of a particular group might lead to the conclusion that there are as many "gods" as there are socio-historical groups. Kaplan denies this, however, by asserting that "the cosmic force of organicity"[169] out of which the idea of God comes is operative in all groups and is the same force or process operative in all groups. "Divinity is that aspect of the whole of nature, both in the universe and in man, which impels mankind to create a better and happier world and every individual to make the most of his own life."[170]

Kaplan speaks of organicity as the notion that the whole affects each part and each part affects the whole. The religion of ethical nationhood implies that the attempt by one nation to lead an exemplary and moral life in which its members can achieve full humanity will affect other nations and groups and finally will affect the cosmos. Organicity also implies that the cosmos is so designed that people can aspire to ever higher levels of human self-fulfillment, because the cosmos is inherently ethical.

Kaplan is building on the insights of modern anthropologists, psychologists, and sociologists when he affirms that it is only in an organic society that a personal ego can be established in the individual. When the group values are internalized by the person as a superego or conscience, the person achieves an even higher level of human existence—an existence which accepts responsibility for oneself and for the group. The religion of a group aids humanity to achieve a higher level of existence. "By holding out or denying rewards and by the exercise of sanctions far beyond the power of any human agency, group religion brings the cosmic awareness, or the awareness of Godhood to the conscious experience of the individual."[171] Awareness of God in this context means recognizing a creative plus in nature or the fact of universal reciprocity. Universal reciprocity means that the natural cosmos is so constituted that it promotes justice, peace, and freedom in individuals and society. For Kaplan, then, there is within the cosmos itself a process that encourages moral character; the natural world is so constituted that values are indigenous to it. Experiencing God means experiencing the ethical nature of the cosmos within one's society and within one's own self.[172]

c. Torah

In his criticism of Reform Judaism, Kaplan emphasized the need for the Torah to be more than a collection of abstract ideas. It needs to be a way of life for a given people. For traditional Judaism this was not a problem because the Torah was the civil law as well as the moral and ceremonial law under which the Jewish people lived. Torah was "the order of social and spiritual life achieved by the Jews."[173] What is needed in our day is a way of life, a Torah, that gives expression and guidance to the values of the modern

Jewish community. "Hence the revaluation of Torah demands that we make Torah synonymous with the whole of a civilization necessary to civilize or humanize the individual."[174] Traditional Judaism saw the Torah as equivalent with civilization, it was a summation of what makes for the good life. If one thinks of Torah not as primarily a book or a document, but functionally, as a way of life, then one can reinterpret Torah in accordance with the needs of the modern day. Torah as a way of life should be something that a people chooses to do, chooses to do because the social customs, laws and standards which it embodies are inherently good. Torah represents a "common purpose to work out a way of life in which each member might conform as a free agent." Torah as civilization points to the fact that a true civilization helps each of its members to achieve life abundant. "All laws, customs, institutions, and social arrangements that hinder the complete self-development of the individual are not civilization, but barbarization."[175] Thus Torah as content is not simply a code of laws. "It is comprehensive in its scope, and includes all the basic elements of human culture." Torah understood as content "embraces a philosophy of life and of history; it outlines a national policy; it prescribes ethical and religious conduct; it lays the foundation of a system of jurisprudence; it deals in matters of etiquettes."[176] In short, Torah covers all aspects of life that would mold a people into a viable ethical community.

Following Durkheim, Kaplan maintained that religion was the expression in dramatic, legal and moral activities of the basic values of a civilization. If this is so, why shouldn't the individual Jew accept the fact that she is part of American civilization, for example, and simply accept as her religion the current value structure of the American nation and thus become entirely assimilated? Orthodox or traditional Jews who still believe in a supernatural God and Torah answer that only by remaining a part of the Jewish community and by keeping all the religious observances can the individual Jew hope to retain a place in the world to come. Integration or assimilation into the life of the host nation would mean losing all hope of life in the world to come. Thus the acceptance of the current value structure of the host nation as a religion is impossible. Kaplan also wants to reject assimilation as the solution for Judaism, but he cannot do so on the basis of a supernatural Torah or God. He does argue that the values that have evolved and which are symbolized in the "sancta" of the Jewish people make it important that the Jewish civilization survive.[177] The heritage of the Jewish people which consists of memories of its past and hopes for its future, a distinct language and literature, the way in which life has been valued that is expressed in laws, morals, customs, and folkways make it important for the Jewish civilization to survive.[178] Further there is the fact of anti-semitism which makes it almost impossible for Jews to find total acceptance from their neighbors.[179] Kaplan makes the point:

> We Jews depend upon Judaism and the fellowship of the Jewish people for that feeling of being needed and welcomed, without which we can neither live a normal healthy life, nor possess the essential ingredients that go into the making of worthy character and personality. We need Judaism to help us maintain our human dignity and achieve our salvation.[180]

As has been noted earlier in this work, Kaplan means by salvation the highest possible self-fulfillment of the individual within a given group. If the Jew cannot be fully accepted by the larger society then there must be some civilization that will make it possible for the Jew to fulfill one's potential as a human being.

d.   "Two Civilizations"

While arguing for the continuation of Judaism as a civilization, Kaplan accepts the fact that the conditions of modern life make it necessary not only for the Jew but for the Christian to live in two civilizations in order to find all the values that a human being needs in order to achieve realization as a human being.

> A way of life that is exclusively American could nowadays be lived only by the American Indian. When the Europeans brought Christianity to this country, they brought a civilization which they have since been synthesizing with those elements of American national life that are the products of the new American physical environment and of the historical events that have created the American people.[181]

Just as the Catholic Christian has had to find ways of cooperating with American civilization so must the Jew learn to live both as part of the Jewish nation and as a part of the American democratic civilization. By finding a way of life in the midst of a larger nation the Jew can help in eliciting "the recognition of a far-reaching social principle, namely that *any civilization which has no aggressive purpose or mission has an intrinsic right to live either by itself, or in symbiosis with any other civilization.*"[182] The Jew who consciously lives in two civilizations will be living by two sets of religious values, because each civilization has its own values arising out of its own historical conditioning and experience. Kaplan sees this as a good.

> Religious hyphenism would, therefore, have to be recognized as legitimate. Nothing better could happen to human life, for that would enable religion to function as a unifying instead of as a divisive influence.[183]

Indeed, if the Jew succeeds in living in two civilizations at once and in giving allegiance to two sets of values the Jew will provide a model for all of humanity. People will have to give up the notion that all religious truth or salvation is found within one definite group, and further will have to give up the idea that nations can only exist in conflict with one another. Just as the modern world has accepted the notion of equality among individuals, it will have to accept the notion of equality among cultural and religious groups. "This means that every cultural or religious group should be permitted to function as the milieu in which the individual's rights to life, liberty and the pursuit of happiness may be realized."[184] Each religious group must give up the notion of superiority of its religion.

> Religious differences do not imply religious inequality, and the assumption that our own religion is superior to all others is no more legitimate than to pretend that we ourselves as individuals are superior to other individuals, or have a superior claim to God's grace."[185]

Giving up the notion of superiority does not, however, mean giving up the importance of the particular group to which one belongs. The individual, while accepting the idea that all religious groups provide salvation for their members, will still be aware that it is in this particular group that this particular individual has obtained salvation or self-fulfillment as a human being.

While working out his "two civilizations" theory, Kaplan found that he could no longer simply reinterpret the notion of the Jews as a chosen people but must abandon it altogether. If one accepts the notion that each group or nation can function as the means of self-fulfillment for its members, and that a person can live in two separate groups, then it follows that no group can claim to be absolutely superior to any other. This is so even if one group claims to be the bearer of grace for all other peoples or groups. As Kaplan says, "The assumption by an individual or a group that it is the chosen and indispensable vehicle of God's grace to others is arrogance, no matter how euphemistically one phrases the claim to chosenness."[186] The Jews cannot consider themselves as a chosen or elect people even if by election is meant that the Jews were elected to bring salvation or the notion of monotheism to the world.[187] However, it is defined, the notion of election implies some type of superiority for the people who claim it. This contradicts the whole spirit and basis of modern democracy. Kaplan has already enunciated the doctrine that a Jew can live in two religious civilizations as long as they do not contradict one another. In order to remain a modern person and live within American society, one must accept the importance and value of democracy. The notion of election flatly contradicts the basis on which democracy is built. "That basis is the intrinsic worth of the individual human soul, a worth which is independent of the people, race or church to which one belongs."[188] Furthermore ethical democracy implies that all peoples, races, and religious groups be regarded as equals in all respects. Election can no longer be considered as a value. It may have had some pragmatic justification in the past as a way of maintaining the cohesiveness of the Jewish people, but in our modern day, when salvation is understood differently, there is no justification for keeping a notion that denies the possibility of salvation to other groups. Kaplan suggests that "vocation" should replace, not reinterpret or revalue, the notion of election. "No nation is chosen, or elected, or superior to any other, but every nation should discover its vocation or calling, as a source of religious experience, and as a medium of salvation to those who share its life."[189]

Not only is the acceptance of equality among groups within a given nation important, a new order of humanity will have evolved when it becomes possible for a nation to live partly as a commonwealth and partly as a distinct

yet integrated group within other nations.[190] Kaplan does not think that Judaism as a religious civilization will be able to survive let alone flourish as a
distinct and yet integrated group within a larger society, such as America,
without intentional action on the part of the Jewish community.[191] What is
needed are for the synagogues, community centers and educational institutions
to constitute the center around which Jewish life in the diaspora revolves.[192]
Further these religious, social, and educational institutions must make it clear
that all Jews belong to "an indivisible people which is a living, continuing
organism, and that it is legitimate for Jews in a democratic society to be part
of that organism."[193]

e.   God

By seeking to interpret both nation and law in functional terms, Kaplan has
tried to preserve that which is of value in the tradition while at the same time
recognizing the changing times in which we live. In *The Meaning of God in
Modern Jewish Religion*, Kaplan focuses on reinterpreting the idea of God in
terms of function. Such reinterpretation or revaluation of the God-idea is not
for him a departure from the Jewish tradition, because even in the biblical age
and throughout the post-biblical age the Jewish people have reinterpreted the
meaning of God to fit the world in which they lived. Thus, ancient Israelites
first thought of God under the image of a bull.[194] Later, the prophets ascribed
to God the attributes of will and thought of God as a person.[195] In the middle
ages, Jewish philosophers like Saadia and Maimonides thought of God as a
monistic essence underlying all things.[196] Kaplan sees himself as part of this
long line of reinterpretation.

Just as the God-idea progressed from a perceptual image to a
conception like the one that identifies God as the sum of all those
factors and relationships in the universe that make for unity,
creativity and worthwhileness in human life, so can the attributes
of God, which once were externalized and concrete be translated
into modern terms and made relevant to modern thinking.[197]

In *The Meaning of God in Modern Jewish Religion*, Kaplan sets out to
do just this, *i.e.*, to translate the attributes of God into modern idiom so that
the term God will be relevant to the needs and thoughts of modern civilization.

With the development of scientific techniques for the utilization of
natural forces, and with the revision of our world-outlook in a
way that invalidates the distinction between natural and supernatural, it is only as the sum of everything in the world that
renders life significant and worthwhile—or holy—that God can be
worshiped by man. Godhood can have no meaning for us apart
from human ideals of truth, goodness, and beauty, interwoven in a
pattern of holiness.[198]

Not even God can escape the limitations imposed on existence by modern
scientific knowledge.

Since God cannot be understood as that which exists outside of nature,
Kaplan proposes that we think of God as the life of the universe or as the
"Power" that evokes personality in persons and nations.[199] In a later work,
Future of the American Jew, Kaplan speaks of God as process, a word that
seems to have the same connotation as "life" does in *The Meaning of God*.
We will speak of the problems involved in defining God as both power and
process later. At this point, however, we will simply pursue what Kaplan
means in speaking of God as "life" and "power." As the creative life of the
universe "God should mean to us the sum of the animating, organizing forces
and relationships which are forever making a cosmos out of chaos."[200] God is
no longer the supernaturally, transcendent being of unlimited power out there

but is instead understood as immanent, as the forces at work within the natural world that make it possible for individuals and groups to achieve salvation. When God is understood to mean not a power outside of nature but that power which is at work within nature, to speak of God as sovereign means to be aware of the forces within an individual nation that are working for social regeneration. All of those forces which contribute to "the establishment of a social order that combines the maximum of individual self-realization with the maximum of social cooperation"[201] constitute what can be meant by God when that term is revalued in order to fit into our modern scientific world view. When the term is revalued to mean the forces at work within society that help individuals and the nation to achieve a more humane existence, it follows that people must be the agents that puts those forces to work for ideal ends. Thus humanity cannot expect intervention by some divine ruler who will make it known how lives should be conducted in order to perfect society. "From the point of view of the sovereignty of God as immanent in human society, the responsibility for ushering in the Kingdom of God on earth rests squarely with mankind."[202]

Thus modern utopias must be those dreams or plans for society for which people are willing to strive and to help bring into existence. Only then can one view life and the life of one's fellow workers as manifesting the divine.[203] Rosh Hashana, from a revalued point of view, marks humanity's willingness to affirm God's sovereignty or to cling to those forces in life that can aid in making an orderly, harmonious society. Modern people must also be aware, to an extent that ancient people could not have been, that the forces of social change can only be actualized through them. The kingdom of God is totally dependent on the willingness of human beings to actively support social change for the betterment of all society. There is no need for a miraculous intervention of Providence or of divine grace in order for the kingdom to come.[204] All that is needed for the kingdom of God to come is for people to study nature and then in accordance with natural law, select those means that will help fulfill the desired social goal—the goal of changing those specific factors in the human environment that will improve man's physical, social and psychological well-being.

Kaplan's practical bent shows through in his discussion of what society needs. By a better society he means better housing, better hygiene, as well as "changes in institutions that determine our economic, political and domestic relations."[205] Social evil is the refusal of a society to so orient its life as to make for the best possible personal development of each individual. Personal evil or sin is the refusal on the part of individuals to live up to the best that is in them.

> If we identify God with that aspect of reality which confers meaning and value on life and elicits from us those ideals that determine the course of human progress, then the failure to live up to the best that is in us means that our souls are not attuned to the divine, that we have betrayed God.[206]

That is to say, we have refused to recognize and to strengthen those forces within us that help us to live up to our potential.

> Whenever we recognize the inadequacy of our acquired personality to do justice to the demands of a new situation, and we try to prevent the obstacles that prevent our lives from manifesting the divine, we are practicing repentance, or the return to God.[207]

Repentance is then a normal part of human adjustment to new situations.[208] Atonement means subordinating the needs and desires of the individual for the sake of the preservation of the ethnic community. The tradition may have been wrong in its way of defining sin as not fulfilling the laws of a supernatural God, repentance as returning to the laws that were commanded by this God, and atonement as making amends for having neglected the law, but the revalued definitions of these terms express in modern terms the basic human needs that the tradition also sought to express.[209]

The underlying Durkheimian influence is apparent in Kaplan's understanding of public worship. He says that in order to experience the presence of God, "it is necessary that we feel strongly our identification with the worshiping community and the totality of its interests."[210] This is so because the term God represents in Judaism, what the term has meant for all civilizations: it symbolizes the highest ideals for which people strive within a given community and further it points to the fact that the world is so constituted that those ideas can be realized. In the last phrase we have that which differentiates Kaplan's view from Durkheim's. Whereas Durkheim sees the term God as merely referring to the projection of humanity's fears, fantasies and desires, Kaplan sees this process at work as a definite process within existence. The world is so constituted that there are forces that transcend human beings, though needing to work through human beings within a given culture, upon which humanity must depend for its existence and self-fulfillment. The term God refers not simply to ideals projected by the human community, but to forces at work in the universe that make it possible for humanity to fulfill those ideals. Here again it should be noted that ideals are not, for Kaplan, supernatural givens but arise out of the needs of people to find self-fulfillment. The ideal society is one in which all human beings can realize their potential as individuals and as members of the group.

For Kaplan, as for Durkheim and Dewey, God is a term which refers to those values which a given civilization or ethnic group most highly esteems. Thus, an individual wanting to understand the term God, must begin by understanding the value structure of a particular society. This is so "because no human being experiences the worth of life apart from his relation to a particular civilization."[211] It is in relation to a particular civilization that a

person comes to accept the particular values that constitute his own salvation.
These values or "the religious element in a people's civilization is objectified
in those institutions, places, historic events, popular heroes, and all other
popular reverence to which superlative importance, or sanctity is ascribed."[212]
For both Dewey and Durkheim the term God referred to the ideal projections
of a given civilization. Kaplan dissociates himself from the notion that God is
simply human projection. He comments favorably on the way in which
Rudolph Otto's conception of a transcendent presence acts as a corrective to
the Durkheimian notion that religion and consequent idea of God grow out of
what a civilization values most highly.[213]

> Actually, these two ways of viewing religious experience supple-
> ment each other. Due to society's impact in the individual,
> religion finds expression in rules of conduct. At first those rules
> deal predominately with ritual and tabus, and only to a limited
> extent with human relationships. In time, the tendency arises to
> reverse the emphasis. Due to the impact of a transcendent pre-
> sence, religion stresses the awareness of that presence as an end
> in itself.[214]

It must be kept in mind that what Kaplan means by transcendent
presence is not the same as what Otto meant by that term. For Kaplan, God
is the transcendent plus within nature and human society; it is not, as it is for
Otto, an independent sacred quality that comes into the phenomenal world
from a transcendent realm. A person finds within a given society powers or a
Power that helps to conquer obstacles toward fulfillment as a human being.
These powers, or power (Kaplan wavers between visualizing the transcendent
as distinct entities and as a unity) are transcendent to an individual and it is
on those powers or power that a person depends for salvation.

Kaplan sees his view of God differing from Durkheim's as well as from
Otto's. Whereas Durkheim would see God as merely the projection of human

fears, fantasies and desires, Kaplan finds a process working for human fulfillment within a cultural context. Religion and culture are inseparable just as Durkheim has seen, but the transcendent plus is God at work within a cultural context. This God is not to be conceived as a magnified human being, but "as the cosmic process that makes for man's life abundant or salvation."[215] God is a real process working within a cultural context. "Belief in God is the intuitive experience of cosmic Power upon which we depend for our existence and self-fulfillment."[216] This belief in God as a transcendent power is the constant factor in religion. The particular conception of God depends on the formulation of a given civilization. Given our modern understandings and world view, thinking of God as process rather than as transcendent person makes more sense and thus makes "God" more real to the modern mind. For Kaplan, the reality of God is as close as one's own personality, because the forces that work for human fulfillment in society also work for human fulfillment within the individual. Thus he can say, "Man's experience of God is as real as his experience of his own personality."[217] The experience of God within human personality does not mean that religion is reduced to a type of humanism. "It differs from humanism in the assumption that man's cosmos is *en rapport* with the human will to salvation."[218] To believe in God is to believe in the organic unity of society and nature and to believe that this organic unity is constituted in such a way that human beings can achieve salvation when salvation is defined as the highest ethical and spiritual achievement possible for humanity. God is the "soul" or divine aspect of the universe that helps in this striving after salvation. Kaplan's God is an impersonal power or process that helps humanity achieve salvation.

Kaplan is aware that to speak of God as impersonal process contrasts with the traditional notion of God as a transcendent personal being. Kaplan wants to speak of forces in the universe that are *en rapport with human* *desi*re to find salvation, and at the same time Kaplan wants to deny that God is conscious. It is difficult, however, to see how one can speak of values as inherent in the cosmos and in human society without thinking in terms of conscious processes at work on the cosmic level. Values are always related to persons. When one speaks of God as a function for human good, one must either equate the good with all the different values of particular human beings or societies or one must ascribe the good to a conscious being that is different from a human person. To say that there is a living universe that is capable of responding to human need for self-fulfillment, suggests at least that the universe has a personal will. It may be anthropomorphic to speak of God in terms of personal consciousness, but to speak of God as consciousless process is to make God of less value than individual persons who not only value certain things but who can be conscious of what they value. To speak of God as a force within the cosmos and within society that is not conscious makes God not more valuable but less valuable than individual human beings. Electricity, to use one of Kaplan's images, may be a great force in the universe, but it is certainly less valuable than the human consciousness that determines how electricity should be used. God, as Kaplan envisions the process, is less exciting and interesting than are ordinary human beings. When God is thought of as an impersonal function within human society, the implication is that God becomes less than, not more than any single individual.

Finally, although Kaplan rejects Dewey and Durkheim's notion of God as projection, his notion that the forces in the universe that make for human fulfillment can only be actualized by individuals or societies means that the divine in the cosmos is dependent on human will and action. For Durkheim, God is the projection of a society's ideals and values. For Kaplan, God is a collective name for forces in the universe that can be utilized in attaining

values and ideals. In both instances, human beings are the determining factor
of what values and ideals shall be obtained. For both systems, the notion of
God as projection, or God as forces that can be used to produce value, are
dependent upon humanity for actualization. And since humans determine the
value structure in both instances, they are thus superior to any force(s) in the
universe that may aid in its actualization.

We see then that one of the basic problems with visualizing God as
impersonal force is the problem of value. Why is something valued? Why is
it better, for example to live in a democracy in accordance with moral and
ethical principles rather than to live in accordance with some other overriding
principle? Why not take power or beauty as a primary principle? Why is it
better for every individual to find self-fulfillment? Is the very constitution of
the forces in the universe—such that they are—determinative of value? If one
answers "yes" then one has to ask in what sense they determine it, and why
are they constituted in such a way as to be friendly to human attempt to find
self-fulfillment? In other words, if the forces are so constituted that they are
en rapport with human values, does that not suggest that there is some
agency beyond human agency that has constructed the universe in this way?
If the universe is so constructed as to allow for and favor humanity's attempt
to achieve salvation, it must follow that the universe, or something that
activated the universe, has something like human will and conscious choice.

Kaplan wants to propose an inherently contradictory notion. He wants to
say that the soul of the universe, the God-process, is favorable to human
values, and at the same time see it as blind forces at work within the historical and cosmological process. Kaplan's God does not decide what is good.
Good is simply a by product of the process which is actualized by individuals. Good refers to that which individuals and societies think of as good.
Yet, in the final analysis, human beings and human societies determine what

is good. To speak of humankind using the forces of nature to actualize good
as divine may be an interesting way of describing the process, but it seems
unnecessary from the logic of Kaplan's system to speak of God at all. Why
not simply speak of persons as using the forces of nature to achieve what
seems good to them within a certain historical and social context?

As was previously mentioned, in *The Religion of Ethical Nationhood*,
Kaplan speaks of the universal reciprocity of the universe.[219] As this writer
sees it, the concept of organicity implies then that there are values in the
cosmos, that the natural order implies an ordering of values as well as a
physical ordering. When using the term organicity as reciprocity between the
parts and the whole as he has done, Kaplan seems to be working out of an
orientation that gives God a character and existence apart from humanity.
From this perspective, God equals all those values that are written into the
nature of things that correspond to the needs and aspirations of humankind.
God in these passages almost takes on the nature of the Aristotelian "lure" in
the universe. Those things which people value are actually part of the organic
structure of the universe. In order for humanity's basic needs for honesty,
courage, and self-fulfillment to be met, those values which are out there must
be actualized within a community setting.

Kaplan ostensibly wants to say two things: (1) that people's basic needs
are creative of value, and (2) that value is inherent in the universe. In the
first instance we have a simple humanism. In the second instance we have
some type of pre-established harmony between humanity and the cosmos, with
humans simply actualizing values that are part of the natural structure. The
question is, can Kaplan have it both ways in the same system? If values are
simply produced out of humanity's need to live in society then values and
hence God are projections, *à la* Dewey. If values are inherent in the cosmos
then Kaplan needs to spell out more clearly why personal needs produce

values that correspond with values that are inherent in the cosmos. If one says that people are so constituted that their needs naturally produce values that correspond with those inherent in the universe, then one has to explain why this is so? Why is there this correspondence? Kaplan's answer that this is just the way it is, that this is the nature of things, is not adequate.

In describing God in functional terms instead of in traditional terms, Kaplan sees a particular similarity between himself and Maimonides. Like Maimonides, Kaplan tries to show how it is possible to retain a particularly religious and Jewish outlook and still be respectable from the viewpoint of the current world view. This is particularly apparent in the way in which they deal with the idea of God. Maimonides was confronted with an Aristotelian world view and found anthropomorphism—the conceiving of God in corporeal form—as the basic problem. Kaplan finds himself in a naturalistic and scientific age. His basic problem, which he deals with at great length in *Judaism Without Supernaturalism*, is the rampant supernaturalism of the tradition. He argues:

> It is high time, therefore, that the problem of supernaturalism in the Jewish tradition be confronted with that frankness, thoroughness, and constructive thinking with which Maimonides faced the problem of anthropomorphism.[220]

By focusing on the way God functions in human life, Kaplan maintains that he is doing in his day what Maimonides did in his, *i.e.*, make the God term understandable to the sophisticated thinker of the day.[221] Throughout the long history of Jewish tradition, belief in God has functioned as an affirmation of life's values. The modern way of speaking of that function is to designate God as a process that works to unify all the values that enhance human existence. By focusing on the way God functions in human life, Kaplan asserts that his theology has much in common with all those theologies that employ the reasoning of the *via negativa*. Like these theologians, Kaplan says that his way of theologizing preserves the mystery of God. Unlike metaphysicians, Kaplan does not have to speak about the essence of God or about what God is in himself. Like modern scientists, Kaplan does not ask the questions of origins or of ends. He need only speak of the way God functions in the world.

> That God, as ultimate reality is unknowable is a commonplace of all thinking other than that which is entirely naive. Theologians constantly remind us that all our affirmations concerning God have to be translated into negatives, if they are to approximate truth. Consequently, religion which aims to improve human nature and the conditions of human living cannot be based on the ultimate nature of God.[222]

The emphasis should be on the here and now. It is fruitless to engage in speculation about the being of God. The rational thing to do is to turn our attention to the ways in which the term God functions in human society.

For Kaplan, God functions as "Power" and process. When speaking of God as "the power that makes for salvation"[223] one is attempting "to identify the particular human experiences which enable us to feel the impact of that process in the environment and in ourselves which impels us to grow and improve physically, mentally, morally, and spiritually.[224] At another point Kaplan says, "God is the Power in the cosmos that gives human life the direction that enables the human being to reflect the image of God."[225] Further, he adds,

> God is that aspect of the cosmos that makes for man's salvation. Man is dependent on God, though God needs man as the sculptor needs the clay or other medium to embody the object of his imagination.[226]

In both of the above quotations, we have the notion of a unified power that impels or that uses people, implying that there is some force outside of humanity that "wills" or plans persons to do something. Yet as we have noted above Kaplan denies any personality to God. In fact, in the same text where he speaks of God as the Power that impels persons, Kaplan speaks of God "as the sum of resources in the world and the capacities in man which, when brought together, enable man to achieve his spiritual welfare."[227] In this case, God is merely a term for a multitude of things that may or may not be related. The question becomes then, is God a determining unity or is God simply an abstract way of speaking about many different entities in the universe? When Kaplan speaks of God as a force that wills or impels individuals, he almost speaks in terms reminiscent of absolute idealism. Accordingly, God becomes the force that moves or creates the universe and human society. When Kaplan speaks of God as the sum of forces, then God is all those natural entities that people can use to achieve their self-enrichment. In the first instance, God is the initiator. In the second instance, God is the sum of the materials that humans use. It is this ambiguity in Kaplan's thought which caused Eliezer Berkovits in "Reconstructionist Theology: A Critical Evaluation," to accuse Kaplan of being both a pantheist and a polytheist. Berkovits says, "The religion of Reconstructionism, is a pantheistic faith of optimism, conceived in a twentieth-century setting, in the traditions of eighteenth-century natural religion."[228] In addition, Berkovits says, "The logic of the Reconstructionist position, however, leads to a modern polytheism."[229] This modern polytheism is not a belief in many gods in the ancient sense but a belief in many processes that help humanity attain salvation, with the only unity among them an abstract unity not an inherent unity.

The ambiguity in Kaplan's thought is carried over into his writing style. At times he uses lower case letters on "powers" and "process" and at other times he uses upper case letters as in the following passage in which he speaks of individuals. "What is most distinctive about himself as a person is termed *soul*, and what is most distinctive about the Power or powers upon whom he depends is termed *God*."[230] In the lower case, "powers" seem to imply that there are things in the world that can be used, just as electricity can be used—simple, natural processes. As "Power" Kaplan seems to be saying that God is more than a simple natural process, or at least a very significant and important process, something that stands apart from and over against humanity. When thinking about God in this sense Kaplan uses the term transnatural. As transnatural, God is "the cosmic process that makes for man's life abundant or salvation."[231] Even as "Power" God does not refer to something that stands outside the natural process but for something that works in accordance with natural law. In this case, at least, it is a unified force.

There is another difficulty in the way in which Kaplan describes God as both power and process. Process as William Kaufman in *Contemporary Jewish Philosophies* points out, implies the notion of development, of God becoming or growing and changing in time.[232] This is the sense that predominates in "Spiritual Leaders for our Day," where Kaplan says, "God means the functioning in nature of the eternally creative process that is forever creating order out of chaos and good out of evil."[233] The concept of Power seems to refer to the energizing ground or source of this movement. On the one hand, we seem to have an emerging deity in the style of Samuel Alexander and, on the other hand, a ground of being such as is found in Tillich.

In *Space, Time and Deity*, Alexander sees God as the next higher level in the emergent or evolutionary process. God is whatever the world evolves into next. Translated into Kaplan's terms, this would mean that the next higher level of value in the emergent process is God. If we think of power as the source of process we come close to Tillich's inexhaustible ground or potentiality for process. Kaplan's thought differs from Tillich's, however, in that for Tillich actualization or stepping out of the ground always connotes fall, whereas for Kaplan actualization is more positively evaluated. Actualization can be steps on the way to greater achievement of value. The process arising from the source is considered salvitic in a way in which it is not in Tillich's system. But just as Tillich finds it difficult to spell out the inherent or necessary relation between the ground and process, between potentiality and actuality, so Kaplan finds it difficult to spell out the relation between power and process.

Henry Nelson Wieman, who both admires Kaplan's work and has independently come to the same conclusions as Kaplan, addresses the problem in the following manner. He identifies power and process because process is always felt as power within human experience.

> Power is process; process is power. Examine any instance of power, such as the explosion of an atomic bomb, or a leader inspiring many men to heroic struggle and utmost effort. What do you find? You always find a process of transformation and nothing else. The individual engaged in action, when such action is called an instance of power, can introspectively be aware of many felt qualities variously called the felt qualities of effort, hope, fear, determination, decision and the like. A streaming flood of felt qualities may pour through his consciousness. But a stream of felt qualities is a process.[234]

Even Wieman, however, is forced to admit that there is a logical distinction between power and process. Process is what we work with and power is what lies behind process. But as experienced, affirms Wieman, they are the same.

Kaplan claims to be following in the footsteps of Maimonides when he rejects the notions of personality and will in his description of God. Maimonides did reject those descriptions of God that give to God a human-like body with arms, legs, and face, but Maimonides does see a correspondence between

God and humans in the realm of spirit or mind.[235] Kaplan goes further than Maimonides in his denial of any resemblance between persons and God. God, he says, "cannot even be viewed as thinking, feeling, or willing in any manner comparable to the way man does."[236] One can speak of God as personal in Kaplan's terms only if one means that God provides the power to help humanity become more fully human. In *Questions Jews Ask*, Kaplan makes the following point:

> The real question is: Does the belief that there is a God make a difference in our personal life? A God who makes a difference in one's personal life should be designated a personal God.[237]

If something makes a difference to me personally, that it then is personal seems to be the logic of Kaplan's thought. God functions in such a way that there is a difference in my life, but God is not, therefore, a person.

In this understanding of God as a function that helps to bring human personality into higher and higher levels of enrichment, but which is itself not a personal being, Kaplan differs from one of his mentors, William James. James's pragmatism, unlike Kaplan's, assumed that a God who has an influence on humanity would have to be personal. For James,

> The more perfect and more eternal aspect of the universe is represented in our religion as having personal form. The universe is no longer a mere *It* to us but a *Thou*.[238]

In the same group of essays where that statement appears, James also says that there are two essential elements to a theistic faith. "First it is essential that God be conceived as the deepest power in the universe; and second, he must be conceived under the form of a mental personality."[239] This personality must also be understood as something distinct from human personality. "God's personality is to be regarded like any other personality, as something lying outside of my own and other than me, and whose existence I simply come upon and find."[240] James's understanding of what it means to speak of God as personal is thus very different from Kaplan's. For Kaplan, God is the ground or process that makes for the growth of human personality; God is not personal.

> If we believe in God as the totality of the influences in the universe which make for our becoming fully human, we must understand by personality that in us in which all those influences are brought to focus.
>
> Personality, understood in that sense and not merely in the sense of the sum total of our mental life, is the manifestation or revelation of the divine. God is thus personal to us, the very ground of our personality. In this sense it is possible to believe in a personal God.[241]

For Kaplan, God is the ground of personality; God is not the other person to whom we relate in dialogue. This differs markedly from James's understanding and emphasis. "In whatever respects the divine personality may differ from ours or may resemble it, the two are consanguineous at least in this—that both have purposes for which they care and each can hear the other's call."[242] Kaplan assumes that there can be no dialogue between God and individuals. God is a process that helps us attain personality, but that process is not personal.

> Choosing, learning, loving are all processes, yet they are all personal; they can only be understood as aspects of the personal life. There is no denying that, in genuine prayer, there is a personal experience of God, but that does not mean that God is a person.[243]

At the beginning of this work it was noted that Kaplan's basic motivation is religious. The problem that his rejection of God as a personal being raises is this. "Can Kaplan maintain his continuity with biblical religion and the Jewish tradition if he denies that God is a person?" In striving to make religion understandable and acceptable to the modern mind, doesn't Kaplan undercut that which is most essential if the Jewish tradition is to survive as religion? Abraham Heschel puts the matter very forcefully.

> If God is a what, a power, the sum total of values, how could we pray to it? An *I* does not pray to an *it*. Unless therefore, God is at least as real as my own self; unless I am sure that God has at least as much life as I do, how could I pray?[244]

Jacob B. Agus makes the same point in "God in Kaplan's Philosophy,"

> Prayer assumes a Being, not a process. We pray to a Savior, a Redeemer, a Liberator, a Father, even to a King.[245]

Kaplan, of course, is interested in the religious life of modern individuals and he defends the viability of his understanding of prayer. "All thinking—and prayer is a form of thought—is essentially a dialogue between our purely egocentric self and our self as representing a process that goes beyond us."[246] Kaplan argues that in prayer we are seeking answers to moral questions. "We seek our answer not from the self that is identified with our appetites, passions and ambitions, but from the higher self, which represents the good of society and, in the last analysis the goal of the Cosmic Process that governs the evolution of mankind."[247]

William Kaufman is very sympathetic to Kaplan's understanding of prayer. He notes that Kaplan's understanding implies that people pray with the creative process and not to the process. In other words, "the function of prayer would be to open ourselves to the creative process as it functions in nature and in us."[248] This comes very close to changing prayer from dialogue to contemplation. To be open to processes in the world, to try to be at one with the cosmos, is very close to what Buddhism means by contemplation, but it is not a dialogue in which one directs a call to the other and the other hears its call, to use William James imagery. James's understanding of prayer comes closer to the traditional understanding of prayer within western or biblical religions. Buddhism may be able to survive on contemplation, but traditions stemming from the Bible have always assumed a conscious will or person to whom prayers are directed. Kaplan's formulation of prayer seems to be striking at that which is central to biblical religions. By eliminating the notion of a personal being, Kaplan has rescued Judaism only by eliminating from Judaism that which is most important.

Kaplan, of course, would reply that he has attempted to revaluate the notion of God so that it will gain new life in the modern world. He is attempting not to undermine the idea of God or religion, but to make these viable options for the cultured and educated Jew. But to do this he insists that the idea of God and religion must arise from the needs and values of a given historic people or nation. A plausible version of Judaism would begin with an attempt to find out what the term God means to contemporary individuals and particularly what this term has meant within Jewish tradition. The focus would be on the ways in which the term God has fulfilled the needs of the Jewish people and made it possible for them to find a satisfying, creative life. The question is not what God demands of the modern Jew, but what function has the term God had within the Jewish community and what function can it continue to have in a naturalistic age. Functionalism does away with all ontological dualisms, whether ancient or modern, whether Plato or Kant. It focuses on the way in which the term God has helped a people to improve itself and live creatively within the world. "Functionalism deals with the relation of means to ends and sheds light upon the *purpose* and *meaning* of human experience."[249] The beginning for understanding the term God is not to look to some transcendent realm but to begin with the basic human needs to find self-fulfillment, communion and spiritual fellowship within a given community. "The idea of the religiously and ethically motivated community is

one of the most significant contributions of the Jewish people to civilization."[250] The religiously and ethically motivated community attempts to remove
all physical, mental, and social handicaps that would prevent an individual
from fulfilling his or her potential, and attempts to "so orient the individual to
his natural and social environment that he shall feel secure and at home in
the world."[251] In other words, one begins with the human need for salvation
and determines that salvation for the Jew means self-fulfillment within the
community. In an earlier age, this meant that the Jew could only attain life in
the world to come as a member of the Jewish community. Today, self-fulfillment must be understood in terms consistent with a natural world view.
Within a modern world view, in order to live a self-fulfilling life within a
community, one needs a religion that fosters "integrity, responsibility, loyalty,
love, courage and creativity."[252] These traits are necessary if a given community or civilization is to provide the best possible life for its people and if
it is going to command their respect and thus encourage their desire to see it
continue. Salvation or human fulfillment on a personal and social scale means
the achievement of these traits.

For Kaplan, the God-idea of any civilization or group is correlative with
what that group sees as salvation. "Whatever constitutes salvation for the
religious community determines the idea of God which the religion of that
community professes."[253] Religious humanism begins with the fact that societies and individuals have certain needs that can only be met in a moral and
ethical understanding of the cosmos.

> When Jewish history and religion are transposed into the key of
> humanism, God is conceived as the functioning in nature of the
> eternally creative process, which, by bringing order out of chaos
> and good out of evil, actuates man to self-fulfillment.[254]

For Kaplan, "God has come to be conceived as that Power in nature and in man which makes for man's this-worldly salvation."[255]

That Power is not a person but a function. As a function, the term God refers to what is done rather than to "who" God is. Furthermore, a function always presupposes a group or entity for whom something is done.

> The term "God" belongs to the category of *functional* nouns. Gold, silver, wood, are *substantive* nouns, but teacher, shepherd, king, are *functional* nouns. A functional noun is necessarily correlative: one is a teacher of a pupil, a shepherd of a herd, a king or God of a people.[256]

God is the Power or structure within human society that makes possible the affirmation of human life and its supreme significance. To believe in God is to believe in the organic unity of society and nature and also to believe that this organic unity is constituted in such a way that people can achieve salvation when salvation is defined as the highest ethical and spiritual achievement possible for humanity.

Each religion should have as its goal the activating of that power in the universe that helps humankind achieve salvation. Ancient Israel experienced God as that creative process which actuates people to self-fulfillment. The Torah which helped people to live in accordance with justice and law aided in bringing about this fulfillment both for an individual and for the nation. Modern Judaism, which is transnational and which should receive its religious focus from the state of Israel, should also accept this mandate to live in accordance with justice and law. The Jews of today need to strive for ethical nationhood, a nationhood not based on political power but on a religio-cultural basis. Like the ancient Jews, modern Jews need to experience God not as a fact but as value. What is needed is not faith in a person or superperson but wisdom to see and try to implement in human life a hierarchy of normative values that will lead to personal satisfaction, social morality, and international peace. From the standpoint of the ancient tradition, it is God who reveals wisdom. From the standpoint of the modern world view, "it is wisdom that reveals God."[257] That is to say, wisdom reveals a hierarchy of values which help individuals attain salvation. In order for a group to attain wisdom, it must recognize "those needs and human values that constitute religious experience."[258] Human needs consist of the following:

> (1) biological needs for health, security and mating, the satisfaction of which is experienced as well-being; (2) psycho-social needs for appreciation and influence, the satisfaction of which yields a sense of power; and (3) spiritual needs, which constitute the human differentia, and which are the needs for controlling and directing human efforts in satisfying biological needs without indulgence in lust and in satisfying psycho-social needs without surrendering to greed.[259]

It is the fulfillment of the spiritual needs that necessitates that life in community. "To satisfy the need for control and direction, the individual requires involvement with his self-governing, self-perpetuating organic community, such as a family, clan, tribe, nation or people."[260] Only through commitment to ethical nationhood can the Jewish people demonstrate to the world how to live in accordance with wisdom. Living in accordance with wisdom makes it possible for a nation to identify as divine "the very processes in nature and in man that function creatively and that make for fulfillment."[261]

Chapter II, Notes

1. Herbert Parzen, *Architects of Conservative Judaism* (New York: Jonathan David, 1946) 22.

2. Mordecai Kaplan, "The Way I Have Come," *Mordecai M. Kaplan: An Evaluation.* Eds. Eugene Kohn and Ira Eisenstein. (New York: Jewish Reconstructionist Foundation, Inc., 1948) 289.

3. Ibid.

4. Ibid.

5. Ibid.

6. Mordecai Kaplan, "Influences that have Shaped my Life," *The Reconstructionist* 8 (June 25, 1942): 30.

7. Kaplan, "The Way I Have Come," 289.

8. Cf. Mordecai Kaplan, *The Religion of Ethical Nationhood* (New York: The Macmillan Company, 1970) 3-4.

9. Ibid., 1.

10. Ibid.

11. Cf. Kaplan, "Influences that have Shaped My Life," 35–36, for a description of the beginnings of the Reconstructionist Movement.

12. Cf. Mordecai Kaplan, *The Meaning of God in Modern Jewish Religion* (New York: Reconstructionist Press, 1962) 9–10, and 19–20.

13. Ibid.

14. Ibid.

15. Kaplan, *Judaism without Supernaturalism*, 26.

16. Cf. Emile Durkheim, *The Elementary Forms of the Religious Life* (1915; New York: The Free Press, 1965) 331.

17. Kaplan, *Judaism as a Civilization* (1937; Philadelphia: Reconstructionist Press, 1981) 333. Durkheim, *Elementary Forms of the Religious Life*, 390.

18. Kaplan, *Judaism as a Civilization*, 334. Cf. Durkheim, *Elementary Forms of the Religious Life*, 321–322 and 324 for a similar exposition.

19. Mordecai Kaplan, "The Law of Group Survival as Applied to the Jews," *SAJ Review* 8 (Sept. 21, 1928): 4; and cf. Durkheim, *Elementary Forms of the Religious Life*, 237–239, Kaplan, *Judaism as a Civilization*, 334.

20. Kaplan, *Judaism as a Civilization*, 335.

21. Ibid.

22. Cf. Durkheim, *Elementary Forms of the Religious Life*, 388–389 and 390 for the importance of the group in a person's moral and intellectual development. Cf. Mordecai Kaplan, "The Chosen People Idea: an Anachronism," *The Reconstructionist* 11 (Jan. 11, 1946): 13–19, where Kaplan repudiates the notion of election.

23. Kaplan, *Judaism as a Civilization*, 335.

24. Mordecai Kaplan, *The Future of the American Jew* (New York: Macmillan Co., 1948) 182.

25. Mordecai Kaplan, "Naturalism as a Source of Morality and Religion," *The Reconstructionist* 29 (Feb. 22, 1963): 9.

26. Kaplan, *Future of the American Jew*, 174.

27. Kaplan, *Judaism as a Civilization*, 394. and Kaplan, *Future of the American Jew*, 174.

28. William E. Kaufman, *Contemporary Jewish Philosophies* (New York: Jewish Reconstructionist Press, 1976) 183.

29. Cf. William James, "Spencer's Definition of Mind," *Collected Essays and Reviews*. Ed. R. B. Perry. (New York: Longmans Green and Co., 1911) 66.

30. William James, *Pragmatism* (London: Longmans, Green and Co., 1928) 200. Quoted by Kaufman, *Contemporary Jewish Philosophies*, 183–184.

31. William James, *Varieties of Religious Experience* (1902; New York: Mentor Books, 1958) 389.

32. Ibid.

33. Mordecai Kaplan, "How May Judaism be Saved?" *The Menorah Journal* 11 (1916): 43.

34. Ibid., 44.

35. Ibid., emphasis mine.

36. Mordecai Kaplan, "The Relation of Religion to Social Life," *SAJ Review* 6 (May 20, 1927): 7.

37. Kaufman, *Contemporary Jewish Philosophy*, 184.

38. Dewey, *Common Faith*, 42.

39. Ibid.

40. Kaufman, *Contemporary Jewish Philosophy*, 184.

41. Kaufman, *Meaning of God*, 89.

42. Ibid., 110.

43. Ibid., 110–111.

44. Kaplan, *Judaism as a Civilization*, 282.

45. Kaplan, "Influences that have Shaped my Life," 31.

46. Kaplan, *Future of the American Jew*, 47.

47. Ahad Ha-Am, "Three Steps," in *Sources of Contemporary Jewish Thought*, no. 1, (Jerusalem, 1970): 53–54, quoted in David Seltzer, *The Jewish Experience in History*, (New York: Macmillan Publishing Co., Inc., 1980), 689–699.

48. Kaplan, *Judaism as a Civilization,* 218.

49. Ahad Ha-Am, "Many Inventions," *Selected Essays of Ahad Ha-Am* (New York: Athenaeum, 1970) 165–167.

50. Ahad Ha-Am, "Priest and Prophet," *Selected Essays of Ahad Ha-Am*, Ed. and trans. Leon Simon (New York: Atheneum, 1970) 132–133.

51. Cf. Ibid., 137.

52. Aaron Arieh Lor, *Processes in Judaism: Ahad Ha-Am and Mordecai M. Kaplan*, (California Institute of Asian Studies, unpublished dissertation, 1975).

53. Unpublished work quoted in Richard Libowitz, *Mordecai M. Kaplan and the Development of Reconstructionism* (New York: The Edwin Mellon Press, 1983), 43.

54. Kaplan, "Influences that have Shaped my Life," 31, also quoted in Libowitz, *Mordecai M. Kaplan*, 43.

55. Ahad Ha-Am, "The Spiritual Revival," *Selected Essays of Ahad Ha-Am*, Ed. and trans. Leon Simon. (New York: Atheneum, 1970) 262–263.

56. Cf. Leon Simon, *Ahad Ha-Am* (Philadelphia: The Jewish Publication Society of America, 1960) 229.

57. Kaplan, *Future of the American Jew*, 36.

58. Kaplan, *Judaism without Supernaturalism*, 188.

59. Ibid., 182.

60. Kaplan, *Meaning of God*, 258, italic emphasis Kaplan's; and cf. "The God Idea in the Problem of Revaluation," *SAJ Review* 8 (October 12, 1928): 8.

61. Ibid.

62. For an interesting historical explanation of this difference in emphasis in their writings, see Samuel M. Blumenfield, "Mordecai M. Kaplan—Ahad Ha-Am of American Jewry." *The Reconstructionist* 22 (April 20, 1956): 10–11.

63. Kaplan, *Meaning of God*, 247.

64. Ibid., 248.

65. Ibid., 248–249.

66. Kaplan, *Judaism without Supernaturalism*, 158–159.

67. It should be noted at this point that Kaplan's interpretation of Ahad Ha-Am's intention may have been incorrect and that there was more agreement between the two than Kaplan realized. On the possibility of all Jews returning to Palestine, Ahad Ha-Am said, "The material problem, on the other hand, will not disappear even after the creation of a refuge, because in the ordinary course of things immigration into the Jewish settlement cannot counterbalance

the natural increase of the Jews in those countries where the majority of them live at present." "The Spiritual Revival," 2.

68. Kaplan, *Judaism without Supernaturalism*, 165.

69. Moshe Davis, *The Emergence of Conservative Judaism* (Philadelphia: The Publication Society of America, 1963) 152–153.

70. Kaplan, *Judaism as a Civilization*, 94.

71. Ibid., 123.

72. Ibid.

73. Kaplan, *Future of the American Jew*, 5.

74. Kaplan, *Judaism as a Civilization*, 124; and cf. Mordecai Kaplan, "Critique of the Adjustment of Reform," *SAJ Review* 8 (March 22, 1929): 21–23.

75. Kaplan, *Judaism as a Civilization*, 117, 121–123.

76. Cf. Dewey, *The Quest for Certainty*, 165–166.

77. Kaplan, *Judaism without Supernaturalism*, 35.

78. Ibid.

79. Don Browning, *Pluralism and Personality* (Cranbury, NJ: Associated University Presses, Inc., 1980) 228.

80. Ibid., 230.

81. Cf. William James, *The Will to Believe and Other Essays in Popular Philosophy and Human Immortality* (New York: Dover Publications, 1956) 11, 20, 205–207.

82. Kaplan, *Judaism as a Civilization*, 134–135.

83. Cf. Kaplan's analysis of Samson Raphael Hirsch's work which is consciously drawn up in opposition to the main tenets of modern thought. Kaplan, *Judaism as a Civilization*, 137–144 and 153.

84. Ibid., 144.

85. Ibid., 142.

86. Ibid., 145.

87. Ibid., 145–146; and see Kaplan's critique of Hirsch on this point in Mordecai Kaplan, "Judaism's Adjustment to the Environment," *SAJ Review* 8 (March 1, 1929): 21.

88. Kaplan, *Judaism as a Civilization*, 154.

89. Ibid., 157–159.

90. Mordecai Kaplan, "Judaism as a Civilization," *SAJ Review* 8 (March 29, 1929): 16, and Mordecai Kaplan, "The Future of Judaism," *The Menorah Journal* 11 (June 1916): 165 and 170.

91. Kaplan, *Judaism as a Civilization* 157–158.

92. Cf. Mordecai Kaplan, "Critique of the Adjustment of Orthodoxy," *SAJ Review* 8 (March 8, 1929): 18.

93. Kaplan, *Judaism as a Civilization*, 145–154.

94. Ibid., 163.

95. Parzen, *Architects of Conservative Judaism*, 189–206.

96. Davis, *Emergence of Conservative Judaism*, 18.

97. Ibid., 13.

98. Parzen, *Architects of Conservative Judaism*, 22.

99. Kaplan, "The Way I have Come," 289.

100. Kaplan, *Judaism as a Civilization*, 160–162.

101. Cf. Parzen, *Architects of Conservative Judaism*, 74.

102. Kaplan, *Judaism as a Civilization*, 161.

103. Ibid., 165. Cf. Ibid., 64; 161–168.

104. Ibid., 167.

105. Kaplan, "Way I have Come," 284.

106. Henry Nelson Wieman, "Mordecai M. Kaplan's Idea of God," *Mordecai M. Kaplan: An Evaluation* Eds. Ira Eisenstein and Eugene Kohn. (New York: Jewish Reconstructionist Foundation, 1952) 210.

107. Wieman, *The Source of Human Good*, 268. Cf. Henry Nelson Wieman, *Intellectual Foundations of Faith* (New York: Philosophical Library Inc., 1961) 177, and *Man's Ultimate Commitment* (Carbondale: Southern Illinois University Press, 1958) 12.

108. Kaplan, *Future of the American Jew*, 183.

109. Ibid.

110. Wieman, *The Source of Human Good*, 77.

111. Ibid., 306.

112. John B. Cobb, *Living Options in Protestant Theology* (Philadelphia: The Westminster Press, 1962), 106.

113. Wieman, "Mordecai M. Kaplan's Idea of God," 203.

114. Kaplan, *Future of the American Jew*, 70.

115. Kaplan, *Judaism as a Civilization*, 47.

116. Kaplan, *Religion of Ethical Nationhood*, 1.

117. Ibid.

118. Kaplan and Cohen, *If not Now, When?*, 14.

119. Cf. Kaplan's argument about the importance of otherworldliness for the tradition in, "A Reply," *SAJ Review* 8 (Feb. 1, 1929): 14–15.

120. Kaplan, *Judaism as a Civilization*, 47.

121. Ibid., 84.

122. Kaplan, *Meaning of God*, 20.

123. Ibid.

124. Ibid., 6.

125. Mordecai Kaplan, "Revaluation of Jewish Values," *SAJ Review* 8 (Sept. 28, 1928): 7.

126. Kaplan, *Meaning of God*, 3.

127. Cf. Mordecai Kaplan, "Judaism as an Unconscious Evolution," *SAJ Review* 7 (March 30, 1928): 16.

128. Kaplan, *Meaning of God*, 3.

129. Ibid., 4.

130. Ibid.

131. Ibid., 5.

132. Ibid., 6.

133. Dewey sometimes uses the word "satisfaction" in the same way in which the word "good" functions in this context. Cf. Dewey, *Quest for Certainty*, 268.

134. Cf. John Dewey, *Reconstruction in Philosophy* (1920; New York: A Mentor Book, The New American Library, 1950) 132 and 141; and John Dewey, *Experience and Nature* (Chicago: Open Court Publishing Co., 1929) 394–404.

135. Cf. Dewey, *Quest for Certainty*, 258–259.

136. Dewey, *Reconstruction in Philosophy*, 147.

137. Dewey, *Quest for Certainty*, 273.

138. Ibid., 310–313.

139. Kaplan, *Meaning of God*, 6.

140. Cf. Ibid., 244.

141. Ibid., 25.

142. Ibid., 46–47.

143. Ibid., 25.

144. Kaplan, *Judaism as a Civilization*, 8.

145. Cf. Kaplan, "On Creeds and Wants." *The Menorah Journal* 21 (April–June, 1933): 44.

146. Kaplan, *Judaism as a Civilization*, 8.

147. Ibid., 235.

148. Kaplan, *Meaning of God*, 92.

149. Ibid.

150. Ibid., 96.

151. Kaplan, *Judaism as a Civilization*, 342.

152. Mordecai Kaplan, "The Relation of Religion to Civilization," *SAJ Review*, 8 (April 12, 1929): 12.

153. Kaplan, *Judaism as a Civilization*, 343.

154. Ibid., 344; and cf. Durkheim, *Elementary Forms of Religious Life*, 469–472.

155. Kaplan, *Judaism as a Civilization*, 259.

156. Mordecai Kaplan, "Can Zionism Reconstitute the Jewish People?" *The Reconstructionist* 29 (October 4, 1963): 14.

157. Kaplan, "The Nationhood of Israel," *SAJ Review* 8 (May 17, 1929): 14.

158. Ibid. Cf. also Mordecai Kaplan, "Paradox—as Witness of the Spiritual," *SAJ Review* 6 (April 1, 1927): 11.

159. Kaplan, *Future of the American Jew*, 125.

160. Ibid.

161. Cf. Mordecai Kaplan, "Aspirations and Handicaps of the Zionist Organizations of America," *SAJ Review* 8 (October 19, 1928): 13–14; Mordecai Kaplan, "Emancipation or Redemption—Which?" *SAJ Review* 7 (April 4, 1928): 7; and Mordecai Kaplan, "Nationhood the Call of the Spirit," *SAJ Review* 8 (May 24, 1929): 20.

162. Kaplan, *Future of the American Jew*, 125.

163. Ibid., 142.

164. Cf. Kaplan, *Judaism without Supernaturalism*, 148.

165. Cf. Kaplan, *Future of the American Jew*, 141–142.

166. The agenda of the Jewish Community organization is in Kaplan, *Religion of Ethical Nationhood*, 147–153.

167. Ibid., 79.

168. Ibid.

169. Ibid.

170. Ibid., 75.

171. Ibid., 83; cf. 78–83.

172. Cf. Ibid., 50, 78, 93.

173. Mordecai Kaplan, "The Revaluation of the Concept 'Torah.'" *SAJ Review* 8 (May 13, 1929): 16.

174. Ibid., 17.

175. Kaplan, *Judaism as a Civilization*, 413.

176. Ibid., 259.

177. Kaplan, *Future of the American Jew*, 46–47.

178. Ibid., 94.

179. Cf. Mordecai Kaplan, "An Antidote to Jewish Anti-Semitism," *SAJ Review* 8 (March 25, 1927): especially 9–11.

180. Kaplan, *Future of the American Jew*, 95.

181. Ibid., 101.

182. Ibid., 102–103, emphasis his.

183. Ibid., 151; cf. 102–103.

184. Ibid., 103.

185. Ibid., 151.

186. Kaplan, "The Chosen People Idea an Anachronism," 14. Also, in *Future of the American Jew*, 219.

187. Ibid., 218–229.

188. Ibid., 224.

189. Ibid., 229.

190. Ibid., 105.

191. Ibid., 118–119.

192. Ibid., 119.

193. Ibid., 121.

194. Kaplan, *Judaism as a Civilization*, 393.

195. Ibid., 359.

196. Ibid., 394.

197. Ibid., 400.

198. Kaplan, *Meaning of God*, 26.

199. Ibid., 102.

200. Ibid., 76.

201. Ibid., 111.

202. Ibid., 119.

203. Ibid., 123.

204. Ibid., 129.

205. Ibid.

206. Ibid., 265.

207. Ibid., 184.

208. Ibid., 181–182.

209. Ibid., 161–162.

210. Ibid., 263.

211. Kaplan, *Future of the American Jew*, 173.

212. Ibid., 46.

213. Ibid., 198.

214. Ibid.

215. Ibid., 183.

216. Ibid., 182.

217. Ibid., 192.

218. Ibid., 193.

219. Kaplan, *Religion of Ethical Nationhood*, 50.

220. Kaplan, *Judaism without Supernaturalism*, ix.

221. Kaplan, *Religion of Ethical Nationhood*, 9.

222. Kaplan, *Judaism without Supernaturalism*, 26.

223. Ibid., 110.

224. Ibid.

225. Ibid., 112.

226. Ibid., 119.

227. Ibid., 202.

228. Eliezer Berkovitz, *Modern Themes in Modern Philosophies of Judaism* (New York: KTAV Publishing House, Inc., 1974) 260.

229. Ibid., 276.

230. Kaplan, *Future of the American Jew*, 171.

231. Kaplan, *Judaism without Supernaturalism*, 183.

232. Cf. Kaufman, *Contemporary Jewish Philosophies*, 206.

233. Mordecai Kaplan, "Spiritual Leaders for our Day," *Reconstructionist* 34 (November 8, 1968): 9.

234. Wieman, "Mordecai M. Kaplan's Idea of God," 202.

235. Cf. Robert M. Saltzer, *Jewish People, Jewish Thought* (New York: The Macmillan Co., Inc., 1980) 407.

236. Mordecai Kaplan, *Questions Jews Ask* (New York: Reconstructionist Press, 1956) 104.

237. Ibid.

238. William James, *Essays on Faith and Morals* (New York: The World Publishing Co., 1962) 58.

239. Ibid., 122.

240. Ibid.

241. Kaplan, *Questions Jews Ask*, 104–105.

242. James, *Essays on Faith and Morals*, 122.

243. Kaplan, *Questions Jews Ask*, 105.

244. Abraham Joshua Heschel, "The Spirit of Jewish Prayer," *R.A. Proceedings* 17 (1953): 162.

245. Jacob B. Agus, "God in Kaplan's Philosophy," *Judaism* 30 (Winter): 32.

246. Kaplan, *Questions Jews Ask*, 105.

247. Ibid.

248. Kaufman, *Contemporary Jewish Philosophy*, 210.

249. Kaplan, *Religion of Ethical Nationhood*, 5.

250. Ibid., 147.

251. Ibid.

252. Ibid., 7.

253. Ibid., 6.

254. Ibid., 10.

255. Ibid., 17.

256. Ibid., 4. And cf. Mordecai Kaplan, "A God to Match the Universe," *The Reconstructionist* 31 (March 19, 1965): 23.

257. Kaplan, *Religion of Ethical Nationhood*, 22.

258. Ibid., 24.

259. Ibid.

260. Ibid.

261. Ibid., 53.

CHAPTER III

BERNARD MELAND

Formative Influences

1. Early Chicago School

It is important to remember that Meland's theological education took place in an institution that had already divorced itself from traditional theological systems and creedal affirmations. The reading of physics, social science, cultural anthropology, and contemporary literature were important ingredients of theological education at the Divinity School of the University of Chicago.[1] In this respect, Meland's theological education was very unlike Mordecai Kaplan's. Kaplan arrived at his rejection of traditional theological systems within an institution that was predominately conservative and literal in its understanding of biblical and traditional materials.[2]

Whereas Kaplan had to strike an altogether different note from his teachers and colleagues, Meland, even with the considerable originality of his thought, was essentially in agreement with the prevailing theological orientation of his peers.[3] For instance, a major concern for Kaplan was the eliminating of supernaturalism from the understanding of Judaism. Meland was freed from this kind of concern, and could turn his attention more readily to the constructive theological task. Meland could assume a general understanding of his writings by his colleagues that Kaplan, at least in the beginning, could not. Whereas Kaplan struggled to introduce the insights of social science into his theological understanding, Meland's task was more to work out the implications of theism within a naturalistic structure that had already in broad outline been established. Kaplan was the pioneer while Meland has deepened and broadened the meaning of theology within a naturalistic structure. Meland's originality comes from the way in which he presses and affirms certain themes. Kaplan's originality stems from the entirely new point of departure for his theologizing.

In an article on the "Early Chicago School," Meland describes the pervasive influence of John Dewey and the importance of a critical study of the Bible. He comments on his own experience under the influence of teachers who had rejected the traditional and literalistic interpretations of scripture. "I was one who literally left the classrooms of Shirley Jackson Case and Edgar Goodspeed transported, having recovered through critical inquiry what had been lost to me through an overweening piety of earlier days."[4] He saw parallels between his own experience and that which his mentors had undergone. "In this I was simply emulating, possibly to a more elated degree, what these critical scholars themselves had experienced in their earlier writings."[5]

The teachers at the Divinity School were not content merely to pursue critical studies in the classroom; they were ardent crusaders reaching out to church groups, colleges, and other groups who they thought might profit from the new knowledge.[6] This crusading mode of existence is also characteristic of Kaplan's thought. In this and in other ways, Kaplan was closer in spirit to the early Chicago School than is Meland. Meland was educated in a climate in which "the (socio-historical) method of interpreting Christian history and the rise of Christian doctrine was pre-eminently an environmental approach to religious thought."[7] These early thinkers at the Divinity School, such as Mathews and Case, "were to derive stimulus directly or indirectly through socio-cultural and historical disciplines such as cultural anthropology, the history of religions, social psychology, and ...sociology."[8]

One needs to be aware of the methodology used by his teachers and its influence on Meland if one is to make sense of the development of Meland's own constructive thought. The teachers at the Divinity School "in seeking to understand the rise of religious ideas and beliefs, moved from the social context in which the group faith had originated, to an understanding of their corporate expressions of faith as speaking out of that formative content."[9] This attention

> to the culture beyond the cultus and to the subtle interrelationship between the two, the inescapable need of any faith to be expressive within the idiom of its time, as well as within its cultural context; not only in order to be communicable and insistent, but in order to survive as a living faith,[10]

became an integral part of Meland's own theologizing.

The methodology of Edward Scribner Ames was most influenced by Dewian functionalism, but all of the faculty of the Divinity School were indebted to it in varying degrees.

> A thing or a movement was known in terms of the function it served. Get at the motives behind actions, affirmations and words, along with the purpose for which they are employed, and you may then unmask the real nature of the event itself. Ceremonials, prayers, beliefs, or doctrines, as well as institutional forms of legislation, were thought to be expressive of "felt needs," as Shailer Mathews was fond of saying. And those needs, in turn, were traceable to a particular complex of environmental and social circumstances or forces.[11]

Meland accepts the importance of culture and the environment in his own theologizing. This is especially evident in *Faith and Culture* where he tried to show how western culture has been shaped by the prevailing Christian mythos. He goes further, however, than either Ames or Mathews in his insistence that there is more than just human and sub-human influences at work in culture and the environment. Even in one of his earliest works, *American Philosophies of Religion*, he aligned himself with Gerald Birney Smith who held, "that belief in God means that there may be found, not merely within the circle of human society but also in the non-human environment on which we depend, a quality of the cosmic process akin to the quality of our own spiritual life."[12] Since for Meland, the mystery of God went beyond what could be articulated simply out of the felt needs of social groups, he sought a method for understanding theology that would do justice to the more diffuse elements of experience. His basic rejection of the scientific instrumentalism of his one time teacher and colleague, Henry Nelson Wieman, centered on the fact that the instrumental approach led to an understanding of "creativity" in which "tenderness and concern that are expressive of the Christian view of God were eliminated."[13] His concern for the sensitive and qualitative elements found within human experience led Meland to develop his notion of the "appreciative consciousness."[14] He saw the "appreciative consciousness" as a counter-balance to the strict instrumentalism that had dominated much of the Chicago School. This appreciative consciousness, which we will discuss at greater lengths later in this work, is the stance that the theologian takes when the theologian is open to all the mystery and depth of experience. It should be noted that Meland is not rejecting the basic naturalism nor the importance of human experience and culture in his theological orientation. He is simply rejecting a method that only concerns itself with that in experience which can be easily delineated and brought into focus. As he says in regards to the modernist movement prevalent at the Divinity School during his student days there,

> Modernism sought clarity of meaning in religion above everything else. In pursuing this effort, one is compelled to say that it misconstrued the nature of the religious response at its deeper levels, dealing with it either as a moralistic or ethical attitude or as an intellectual decision in value.[15]

For Meland, this emphasis impoverished religion. It impoverished it in at least three ways. This emphasis suppresses emotional intensity, ignores appreciative awareness, and neglects the tragic sense of life.[16]

As early as 1934 in "The Appreciative Approach in Religion," Meland spoke out against a theological method that modeled itself so completely after science. "Theologians have been as eager as the social scientists to become scientific in the sense of being able to establish objective criteria for defining religious values."[17] This is a mistake. Meland continues:

> Theologians must reckon with the fact that their intellectual undertaking is motivated by objectives that differ decidedly from those of the scientist. The scientist pursues knowledge of his world with a view to controlling and using its processes.[18]

The theologian's purpose is not to control but to evoke worship. For Meland, "Worship in its supreme moments may mean indescribable contentment with God—friendly commerce with the whole of existence, wholly apart from any thought or intention of using God or reality for ulterior benefits to one's self."[19] It is because the theologian is primarily interested in worship and not in function or use that there is the need to take art and poetry as seriously as science and logic. The theologian needs to begin with a method that can probe the depths of experience. The theologian needs to begin with a method that takes seriously the immanence of God.

Meland sees himself as carrying on the tradition of naturalism inaugurated by his teachers at Chicago. Thus for all his differences from his mentors, he sees himself as working within a decidedly American idiom. Though several of his teachers had studied in Europe, they never patterned their theological or philosophical method after European models. Meland describes the Early School at Chicago in the following manner. "I would say that these young scholars of the early Chicago School either abandoned what they had begun in Europe, or turned what they had acquired as a disciplined mode of study to contemporary ends within a medium native to the American experience."[20]

In his own case, even though he studied under Rudolph Otto and produced his *Modern Man's Worship* shortly after his return to the United States, he found that the main impetus for his work did not come from the liturgical reforms surrounding Otto and his followers, but "was prompted initially by what was referred to among British and American scholars in physics, philosophy and religious studies as "the new mysterious universe."[21] This new mysterious universe emphasized "theories of relativity and a space-time imagery of relations."[22] Although he subsequently incorporated some of the European experience into his work, he was always conscious that his own concerns were different from those of the European theologians. He saw himself as addressing issues that arose from taking seriously the possibility that God was part of the natural world in which human beings live. As he says,

> My *Modern Man's Worship* was initially projected in my own thinking and addressed to that new realistic vision of creature-hood, stressing a sense of at-homeness in the universe, but in a universe which had just been disclosed as being more mysterious, yet at the same time, more amenable to our creatural ways, and sustaining of its existence.[23]

In spite of the naturalistic orientation of his thought, Meland does differ decidedly from the modernists of the Chicago School, such as Mathews, Case and Ames. These men emphasized "functional adaptations in response to the demands of a changing environment and the forward-solving perspective consequent to it."[24] This Darwinian influence in theology led to the neglect of any ultimate dimension. Only the present and the controllable future need be explored. As long as their theology "attended to the immediacies of nature or experience, no ultimate questions need intrude or be considered."[25] Meland points out that they could do this because an unexpressed tenet of their methodology was the belief that the evolutionary process itself guaranteed an increment of value and good in the world. Meland comments on these teachers in the following way, "Sanguine modernists could accept this dismissal of ultimate questions because their faith in the evolutionary process was such that they need have no fear of its implications."[26] In "From Darwin to Whitehead" Meland makes this comment on the modernists' method.

> The Chicago School of theology made much of its opposition to philosophical idealism; but its strategy of thought in transmuting evolution into something other than mechanistic naturalism was actually dictated and directed by the vestigial remains of their own personal idealism. It could hardly be otherwise, with environmentalism and functionalism playing so large a role in the formulation of their critical method. There was nothing in the method itself to justify a religious or a Christian resolution of problems that emerged. Some recourse to idealism, as a counterpart or corrective of the mechanism implied in its environmental and functional method, was demanded, whether implicitly or explicitly employed.[27]

Meland, following the lead of Gerald Birney Smith, wanted both to ask ultimate questions and to do so within a naturalistic setting, without having to have recourse to hidden assumptions. To do so, however, required a re-thinking of that naturalistic setting. This led Meland to take seriously the works of William James, Henri Bergson and Alfred North Whitehead.

The genius of the empirical movement as Meland saw it was that it took the temporal process seriously. History was important. Unfortunately in liberal Protestantism, historical experience became equated with social experience and that contracted into practical experience. Religion became restricted to ethical decision and the focus was on activism and ethical control of social groups. The most fundamental aspects of lived experience became "work, action, industry, force."[28] For Meland, this way of understanding experience was too restricted. He suggested that a preliminary step in initiating "a more adequate conception of the living process"[29] would begin with the bringing together of two sources of wisdom, one ancient and one new.

> The ancient one is the imaginatively conceived events of biblical history which myth-makers, poets, prophets and seers portrayed; the new source is the recent metaphysical literature which centers all philosophical concern in an explication of the creative passage of events, or creativity.[30]

Taken together these two strands of wisdom pointed to a qualitative depth, a more in experience, that went beyond the practical and functional. These two strands widened the notion of experience to include the aesthetic and ultimate dimensions. Meland agreed with his teachers that the immediate situation was important, but he attempted to broaden and deepen what could be conceived as the immediate situation.

2.   Influence of the Philosophers

Drawing upon James, Bergson and Whitehead, Meland attempted to reconceive the immediate situation. The focus is still on the immediacies of the present situation, but the present situation is understood not only along objective and functional lines, but in terms of depth and in terms of relations as internal and experienceable. At about the same time that Newtonian science was made obsolete, Henri Bergson and William James "were introducing into philosophy and psychology, respectively, the notion of relations as being internal and experienceable which was to alter radically the terms of philosophy laid down by Descartes, Kant, and Hegel."[31] Whitehead, working within the imagery of the new physics, was to make explicit the notion that relations were experienced both as objective and internally.

Meland does not deny the reality of cultural groups and social structure, but the objective phenomenon is not the whole of experienced reality. Bergson intrigued him because the French philosopher took with utmost seriousness and attempted to express through his notion of intuition that there is a depth to lived experience that is missed by objective and abstract modes of thought,[32] and he attempted to express this through his notion of intuition. Meland accepted this emphasis of Bergson, but he thought that Bergson failed to do justice to the fact that these internal relations also formed an external pattern of relations. James went further than Bergson and called attention to the thickness or depth of experience, by which he sought to suggest that our perception of relations refers to both the external and internal situation.[33] The doctrine of prehension, which was finally enunciated by Whitehead, tried to do justice to both external and internal relations, to both "structured meaning in the creative flow of the living situation"[34] and to dimensions of depth that go beyond structures amenable to cognition. Meland spoke of Whitehead's notion of prehension in the following way.

> Subject-object are not too sharply differentiated entities that may be conveniently or arbitrarily treated as separable; but stand in a context which is itself integrating. In any act of perception, the living emotion which attends the apprehension of any object is a relevant part of the datum in understanding the object itself. It cannot be "abstracted from the bare intellectual perception." On the other hand, the bare intellectual perception which is implied in the conscious discrimination of all descriptive analysis—in psychology as well as in physics, in philosophy and philosophy of religion that pursues a positivistic course—cannot be sustained as

adequate description. For "all perception," as Whitehead said, "is clothed with emotion."[35]

For Meland this reconceiving of the empirical situation meant that one was not only allowed to describe group functions and social structures, it also allowed for the perception of ultimacy and transcendence within the historical, empirical situation. The emphasis on social structure led to taking humanity and its ideas seriously. The emphasis on qualitative influences within the empirical experience led to a consideration of that which was beyond human realms. In *Higher Education and the Human Spirit*, Meland contrasts James's understanding of the empirical situation with that of Dewey. Dewey focused on discernable social groups and functions while James pointed to the less discrete qualities that are also there in the empirical situation.[36] Meland later elaborated on James's position saying, James's

> chief bent of mind and interest was that of probing possibilities of attending what he called the "more" in experience which eluded perceptual experience in most instances, but which, in any case, could be only meagerly assimilated to experiences of the most sensitive and perceptive individuals.[37]

Dewey's functionalism led him to the conclusion that human consciousness is the summit of existence. God becomes an ideal construct of the human mind that is a plan for action. James's method led him to an understanding of God that went beyond what was possible for the human. For James, "the knowing mind, the seeking mind, moves in a world of pure experience which continually confronts the human consciousness with intimations of a good not its own."[38]

From Meland's point of view this good that transcends the human spirit and consciousness is not totally unrelated to it.

> The nature of this human consciousness, the nature of the data to which mind and feeling are attuned partake of a different quality,

pointing, so it seems, to a different order, yet not to a different order in the sense of its being utterly opaque or transcendental in meaning.[39]

Meland finds the analogy of levels as understood by the emergent evolutionists helpful in trying to express what he means. Each level in the emergent evolutionist's schema is both a decided break with what comes before and after it, and yet each level has similarities to that which comes before and that which follows.

> Emergence implies a reconception of all evolutionary thinking. Though it holds to the theory of more complex structures arising from simple ones, it by no means concurs with the notion that therefore these complex structures are reducible to the simple material levels. There is continuity of a sort between the various levels of structures; but there is also discontinuity of a significant sort.[40]

In the same way, it can be said, that the individual's level of being both partakes of structures common to both humanity and God and is transcended by God. For Meland, the individual can perceive the workings of God in nature and in culture and in experienced individual life, but perception never means total comprehension. God always remains a mystery.

Meland was greatly excited by Whitehead's works. He understood these works, however, not as a literal description of existence but as a poetic analogy of existence.[41] Understood in this way, Whitehead seemed to him to be extending and amplifying some of the basic intuitions that were found in Bergson and James. Moreover, it seemed to him that Whitehead's emphasis on feeling upheld that which was basic to Protestantism.

> Whitehead's thought is a metaphysics of feeling and ultimately justifies the appeal to man's total nature—a presupposition that is implicit in all Protestant thought and accounts for such emphasis as "the primacy of faith" and the appeal to religious experience.[42]

For Meland, Whitehead offered a cognitive structure for Protestant thought that was a promising alternative to Thomism.[43] This deep appreciation for the insights of Whitehead's thought did not cause Meland to be blind to its limitations. Whitehead's work was an illuminating and suggestive reading of experience. It was not, for Meland, however, a literal reading of experience.[44] Meland saw that Whitehead's imagery, which was derived from the new physics, emphasized a structured meaning in the creative flow.[45] This emphasis, which insisted that meaning was out there, as well as in the perceiving mind, made it less likely that Whitehead would be charged with subjectivity than Bergson and James. On the other hand, there was a real danger that disciples of Whitehead would understand his thought as more external and rationalistic than Whitehead meant it to be.[46] After making the point that there is a depth to lived experience that cannot finally be put into propositions, Meland says,

> It was this that Bergson knew well and meant to take with the utmost seriousness and realism. The followers of Whitehead who take his imagery literally without pondering this important insight are inclined to be more rationalistic than Whitehead intended, and than the method of rational empiricism requires.[47]

It is to passages like this that Ty Inbody refers in his assessment of Meland's relation to Whitehead and process thought.

> I would propose...that Meland is a process theologian in the sense that he accepts and employs the process metaphysical vision and scheme as a backdrop of his thinking, but that he is distinctive among process theologians in his understanding of the cognitive status of the vision and selective in his use of the scheme.[48]

Meland himself is very aware of the selective use which he makes of Whitehead and other process thinkers. In an article aptly entitled, "Interpreting the Christian Faith within a Philosophical Framework," these words appear,

The picture which the topic of this discussion quite naturally suggests is that of one attempting to compress his Christian affirmation within a rigid framework of propositions defining certain basic categories. I must warn my readers at the outset that I have no intention of attempting so arbitrary a task. Ordinarily, in fact, were I not assigned to examine the possibility of interpreting the Christian faith within an acknowledged structure of thought, I should prefer, in setting forth my affirmations of faith, to have these conceptual matters work on more hiddenly.[49]

Meland allies himself with the tradition stemming from Augustine when he says,

Faith precedes and underlies the structure of philosophy, in the individual as in the culture. This is certainly true in my case. The Biblical drama of redemption, from the Exodus to the Cross and the resurrection of Jesus Christ, forms the earliest chain of childhood images of which I have any conscious recollection.[50]

Meland did not go from a philosophical understanding to an appreciation of the Christian faith, nor did he try as a mature thinker to put his Christian faith within a philosophical framework. As he says,

philosophical orientation is more in the nature of a structure of mind and feeling which forms the depth of my conscious experience and which brings to play upon the accumulations of experience, insight and brooding upon the problem of faith, the full light of day, the sustained view, because the discrepancies, the broken meanings, the fragments of faith, the hit-and-miss turnings of thought which had no connectedness, no order, no symmetry, could now assume a pattern of relationships.[51]

While denying that his faith is dependent on his philosophical understanding, Meland admits that his thought owes much to Whiteheadian metaphysics.

The perspective in which my thought moves is that which is being pointed up these days by what is frequently termed "the new metaphysics." This new metaphysics, which is simply the new vision of the sciences imaginatively informed and elaborated, partakes of "field theory" in its various aspects along with the notion of emergence.[52]

From this "new" metaphysics Meland selects five fundamental notions that are particularly important in his constructive theological statement. (1) *Events are primary.* An event is "the simplest form of existence beyond which no analysis of event can go, and in its ultimate sense inexhaustible: the bearer of all that is in miniature."[53] (2) *"God in his concreteness is a sensitive awareness at work in every emerging event which accounts for qualitative attainment in existence."*[54] God is that matrix of sensitivity "in which all life is cast and out of which all structured events arise."[55] It is God's act within the process that turns what would otherwise persist as brute force into events with direction, with capacity for a sensitive response, for selection, for decision; in short, for "feeling and sensibility in all their range of meaning."[56] (3) *Reality is social in character.* "The fact of sociality derives from God's intent as Creative event in which individuals are created in community."[57] Within the communal context individuals are lured on to fulfillment by "a persistent impulse of love within the power context of process."[58] For Meland, God both initiates the process and acts as a gentle persuader within the present moment, leading the world to higher levels of sensitivity and complexity. God is both the ground of being and the goal of existence. Accordingly, "the social nature of reality applies both to the ground of being and to the goal of emergence in so far as one may speak of a definitive end of existence."[59] (4) *Relations are dynamic.* A static reading of events, whether it be of human thought in an individual consciousness or of words in a sentence, is a falsification. Any abstraction is a reading of the past (either of the recent or the distant past), but it is impossible to grasp the living essence of events in static categories. It may be necessary to abstract from the total flux in order to achieve manageable blocks with which to work, but the abstractions never embrace the full complexity and depth of the lived situation.[60] (5) *The possibility of emergence accompanies each structure.* "Relations are thus seen to suggest not simply the notion of pattern but the interaction of structures in a way which makes for a subtle progression from lower to higher organizations of events."[61] The subtle progression from lower to higher levels of organization carries with it an advancing sensitivity of structures. Mystery and promise are attendant on each actualized level of existence.

These five notions occur over and over again in Meland's theological construction, but Meland rejects the suggestion that in using these notions he is attempting to provide a philosophical structure for the Biblical and traditional materials of the Christian faith. "Rather it is to be understood simply as the witness of the Word reaching the structured mind in ways that are intelligible to disciplined perception."[62] The structured mind can both receive the witnessing Word and be broken and re-created by that witness. Here again we see the recurring insistence that no philosophical system, not even the one with which Meland is most sympathetic, is the final or indisputably best system for interpreting the Christian faith. All systems are conditioned and finite and are capable of being superseded by new insights and perceptions of what is good.

Whitehead is important to Meland both because of the empirical base of Whitehead's system and because of the way in which Whitehead understands and incorporates aesthetics. In his system we see the mingling of a genuine sensitivity of spirit and a relentless bent for scientific-rational inquiry.

> Whitehead's use of poetry in carrying on a metaphysical discussion is an example of how these two dimensions of mind can intermingle, enabling the mind to act definitively and yet be inclusive toward imaginative meanings which in the nature of the case resist a precise handling.[63]

Meland not only applauds the use of poetic imagery and expression in Whitehead's system, he understands Whitehead's entire system as a poetic vision, an imaginative generalization of what the world would be like if it could be seen whole.[64] The system is a grand vision which is closer to poetry than to a literal reading of reality. For Meland, metaphysics, like poetry, "creates overtones and backdrops of coloring in scenes that might be descriptively drab or shorn of extending dimensions. When poet and metaphysician work, they employ a medium that goes beyond description, beyond literalness and exactness."[65]

Relation to the European Tradition

With the new understanding of empirical as referring to relations and not to discrete data, Meland saw an increased possibility of taking seriously the Christian affirmation that "God is with us" concretely at work in the world. His main criticism of Barth and Brunner and even of Tillich was that each of these figures, in his own way, downplayed the importance of God's immanence.[66] Barth's despair over the empirical situation and Tillich's ability to only see questions or problems within culture seemed to Meland to underplay the elements of grace and goodness that were part of the empirical situation.[67] At first he viewed Barth's work, and Brunner's also in so far as the latter depended on Barth, as an attempt to re-assert the claims of the old supernaturalism at the cost of cutting theology off from all the new discoveries in physics, anthropology, sociology and metaphysics.[68] Later he was to suggest that both theologians used a method similar to that of the language analysists; that is to say, they both drew their imagery from a formal pattern making their theology "no longer continuous with concrete facts of existence."[69] Further, they theologized from this formal pattern in a literal way that obscured the difference between mythical meanings and concrete meanings. In both his earlier and later interpretations of the Continental theologians, his basic criticism is the same. They fail to take seriously the empirical situation as a source of grace.

While recognizing these major differences between himself and the European theologians, Meland saw himself allied with them on certain key issues. In "The Mystic Returns" published in 1937, he noted that the naturalistic theist and the Europeans rejected the liberal quest for specific character traits that could be learned by those wishing to become Christian.[70] Jesus could not be a model for people's life in the simple manner presupposed by early liberalism. Both the American naturalist and the Barthian theologians sought to undercut the subjectivity of liberalism in order to relate humanity "to a wider context of reality."[71] In order to do this, the theological naturalist looked for help from insights gained from anthropology, physics and the new metaphysics. "The Barthian, less attentive to metaphysics and the natural sciences, seeks to recover the objective phase through a renewed emphasis upon revelation—a supernatural realm."[72]

Another place were Meland saw his theology and the Barthians' converging was in the attempt to re-orient life so that it is God-centered and God-controlled. Both stressed the distinction between creature and Creator and both emphasized God's transcendence. They rejected the old liberalism that "implied such intimacy between God and man as to give the impression that man, in his fullness as creature, is really God."[73] Meland envisioned God as working creatively within history. He saw "faith as a deeper rapport with the life process and with the living God, who is creatively at work within its events."[74] The empirical theist, in seeking to work within the framework of natural experience, intends to push beyond the merely human to a perception of that which is superhuman and transcendent within the empirical situation. Barth's initial speaking of God and goodness as eternity breaking into time seemed to Meland to be simply a return to the old supernaturalism and thus left Barth at an impasse when it came to dealing with the modern world.[75] Barth had won a transcendent God at the price of making God irrelevant to the thought-world of modern individuals.

Another general area of agreement between the Europeans and Meland was their view of human limitations. They both emphasized "the unworthiness of humanity and the need of penitence, discipline and redemptive change."[76] They both took with renewed seriousness the depth of human evil, seeing this evil as more than simply a vestige of the pre-human animal nature that the evolutionary process would automatically overcome. They both saw a crisis in the present culture that stemmed from the over-emphasis on individualism at the expense of the need to relate to God and to other human beings. There were significant differences in the Continental and American assessment of human nature, however. The Continental theologians regarded humanity as utterly impotent and culture as totally devoid of God's presence.[77] The American empiricists tended to characterize humanity as inadequate by itself to live a fulfilled life, to save itself or the world. Against the Continental theologians stress that one can know nothing of God and is thus totally dependent on the revelation in Jesus Christ known through the scriptures, the American naturalist insists that one can and does know something of God within human experience and culture. From Meland's perspective, the Continental theologians insistence that Christ alone is the mediator of God's grace "makes for the complete depreciation of all structures of value that are in any sense continuous with experience."[78] Jesus Christ is from this moderate Christian stance the focal point of the God-man relationship, but this does not rule out the fact that God is still at work in the natural and historical world.[79] Indeed, Meland sees this total dependance on Christology as itself based on a certain assessment of the empirical evidence. "Grace is seen as wholly other than these structures of experience because experience itself has become so devoid of grace."[80] Meland admits that "faith as a structure of experience is supported by fragile fibers,"[81] but "Christ is a datum of the concrete experience."[82] This Christ is "as Whitehead has intimated, an eruption in history in which the good that is in God and the tenderness of mere life itself came visibly to view."[83]

His understanding of God as part of the empirical reality means, for him, that all peoples and cultures have some intimation of God's presence.[84] Thus Meland rejects Brunner's attempt to dissociate the Christian myth from all non-Christian myths,[85] and he repudiates the attempt to speak of the Christian myth as essentially different from other religious myths. For Meland,

> myth is a characteristic human response in any situation where the human psyche is awakened to a disturbing realization of an otherness, either in the form of a single object of power, or in the form of a total datum, affecting or determining man's present existence as well as his future destiny.[86]

Meland does not suggest that this means that all myths are equal, nor does he attempt to arrange them in a serial order. He does see the need "to recognize that comparable human responses in the way of being expressive and creative lie back of the cultural motifs to which the various myths have given form."[87]

Even though Tillich's apologetic theology has taken the data of culture more seriously than has either Barth or Brunner, Meland still finds a radical separation between the divine and the natural world; a separation which from Meland's position does not do justice to the Christian doctrine of immanence, nor to the concrete empirical situation. Meland sees Tillich's thought as depending on Platonic imagery. There is a spirit world or ideal world that casts its shadow "or its illumination upon natural structures, giving to them a transcendent glow or spirituality."[88] This gives to Tillich's work a different context of meaning than is presupposed in empirical realism.

> For what is presupposed in empirical realism is not that reality casts its shadow or transcendent light upon natural structures, giving them the appearance of spirituality, or fleeting encounters with it, but that these immediacies of concrete experience actually participate in the depth of the Creative Passage in which the human structure of sensory life is integrally related to other structures, and to what is genuinely ultimate as a dynamic of creativity.[89]

For Meland, God is that gentle force at work within nature and human experience. Tillich's way of understanding seems to undercut the reality of God in history. Correspondingly Tillich, like Barth and Brunner, undercut the reality of religion as part of the contemporary, experienced world, while the American theologian envisions "a religion that enters creatively into the life and spirit of current humanity."[90]

Meland admits that from one perspective cultures can be viewed as "powerful and potential obstructions to God's working, and tend to become aggressively hostile to His working by reason of their corporate arrogance, their autonomous pride, or simply their insensibility."[91] Even in the most unpromising situation, however, Meland insists that "the concrete facts of the situation reveal subtle connections between God and culture by reason of the actualization of tenderness and sensitivity in specific human groups, in specific structures of human consciousness."[92] He quotes Abraham's words to God "If there are ten righteous, I shall not destroy the city," as an apt parable on the human situation. "Existence," as he says, "in most instances is sustained by a perilously slight margin of sensitivity."[93] However slight the margin of sensitivity, this margin is for Meland an indication of God's work in history. He says,

> To speak of God's operations in history as a tender working is not to reduce it to sentiment which may or may not be ignored; it is rather to speak of it as a subtle, intricate, disciplined, restraining, resourceful, persistent, patient, and deep-working process, not unlike the skill of the artist's hand, that shapes the crude clay into visible structures of beauty and intelligibility.[94]

For Meland, God is not above or beyond time and culture, but is that sensitive working within time and culture that gives meaning and direction to both.

Relation to Contemporary Empirical Theologians

1.   Wieman

Meland co-authored *American Philosophers of Religion* in 1936 with Henry Nelson Wieman. Meland was both appreciative of Wieman's work and yet distanced himself from Wieman's approach at certain crucial points. Like Wieman, Meland considered himself a religious naturalist. Like Wieman, he came to reject any attempt to equate humanity and God. In *The Reawakening of the Christian Faith*, Meland notes that Wieman was at one with Barth and the continental theologians in rejecting the subjectivity of early liberalism. "Every tendency to identify religion or God with human ideals or values drew from Wieman a sharp rebuff."[95] In *Faith and Culture*, written twenty years later, Meland continues and strengthens the argument against religious liberalism which made God simply continuous with human consciousness. Wieman thought it folly to suggest that humanity could save itself. The question Wieman posed for himself was how one could validate the workings of God within the empirical situation. He wanted a method that would give him as much certainty as the Continental theologians claimed to derive from revelation. His solution was an appeal to scientific method by which he meant cooperative inquiry. "Tested knowledge, such as emerged from cooperative inquiry, he contended, did not carry the limitation which he, along with Niebuhr and Barth, attributed to human reason and subjective experience."[96] Wieman held that cooperative inquiry guarded against the unconscious drives and compulsions that ruled individual thinking. Cooperative inquiry guaranteed a minimum degree of certainty, but for Wieman that minimum degree of certainty was all important.[97] What cooperative inquiry revealed when it focused on the Christian tradition, as he saw it, was "the structure of events that has been, is now and will forever be creative of good."[98] Meland has pointed out that the degree of certainty which Wieman found through this method really did not allow him to assume that the structures that were operative for good in the past or in the present, so far as they can be discerned, will be operative in the future. The hidden assumption on Wieman's part was that history is moving on toward higher and higher structures of good, but there is nothing in the method of cooperative inquiry, as such, that validates that assumption. Meland believes that the Absolute Idealism of Royce and Hocking persists in Wieman's thought. He retained "a vision of an ultimate reality, cosmic in scope, which somehow commanded adjustment and, in turn, provided resources for human growth and fulfillment."[99] This vision obviously goes beyond what a strict empirical method of cooperative inquiry can reveal, and yet Wieman clings to this method as a way of providing certainty for his religious affirmations. Meland believes as wholeheartedly as does Wieman that God is immanent, i.e., working within the natural-historical context, but he rejects the scientific method as the method whereby God's working can be perceived.[100] He finds Wieman's search for clear and distinct patterns within the empirical situation as a type of logical positivism; Wieman abstracts his data from the total relational context and thereby fails to take account of the richness and mystery that goes beyond clarity in the historical situation.[101] Meland does not deny that there are patterns of values and structures in the world that promote good.[102] What he does deny is that one can so unambiguously sort out what these patterns are, and he is convinced that focus on value leaves out the aesthetic and creative dimensions of existence.[103] Meland concludes that Wieman's model of empirical observation and verification depends on a vision of the world that is closer to Locke and Newton than to the vision of the world enunciated by Einstein and Whitehead.[104] Like Locke and Newton, Wieman's method presupposes a static universe and a stance outside of it from which the ego can view it. Einstein and Whitehead, on the other hand, insist on observation and verification chastened by relativity theory; the individual viewers are always conditioned and limited by their own perspective and there are always unmanageable depths in reality that elude their grasp. In *Realities of Faith*, Meland says this in regards to Wieman.

> While his view of history conveys the complexity of events, seen in relation to depths of creativity, his method of inquiry results in isolating a specific structure of meaning as being normatively expressive of that depth, and thereby tends to foreclose the import of what is unmanageable and hidden in the depth of historical realities.[105]

2.   Hartshorne

If Wieman searches for theological certainty through scientific method, Charles Hartshorne, although working out of an empirical context and seeking to provide a structure that explains human experience, pushes analogy to the point that the gap between imagery and reality is obscured. This is clearest in Hartshorne's discussion of the "logic of perfection" by which he seeks to prove that if God is a necessary presupposition in order for human experience to make sense and if human experience does not contradict that notion, then in fact God must exist.[106] Now, as long as Hartshorne simply means that, given the initial premises, this makes good sense metaphysically, there is no quarrel between him and Meland. Meland, however, thinks that Hartshorne means more than this. "Hartshorne, in other words, would appear to be bent on precision and perfection of conceptual statements in the sense in which *picture-models* can be presumed to provide descriptive clarity in an ultimate, rather than a provisional sense."[107] In this respect, Meland sees Hartshorne as going beyond even Whitehead in his identification of reason and reality. The result "of this strong, rationalistic bent of mind is to presume more security and certainty in religious belief than human judgment is entitled to affirm."[108] Both Wieman and Hartshorne reveal a trust in human intellectual powers that transcends what is possible given the finitude and relativity of human beings. Taken as parables about God or ultimate reality both Wieman and Hartshorne have provided us with powerful statements. But these statements and pictures are not what is real. The human situation is such that *at best*, through the most disciplined and persistent efforts, with adequate sensibility as to what is beyond comprehension, conceivably beyond our apprehension, we may aspire to a degree of intelligibility and encouragement to persist in the act of faith in a mood of openness to such intimations of insight beyond the assured sense of intelligibility as these lived experiences may yield."[109]

Because of his lack of trust in human capabilities, Meland avows that language is never adequate to describe reality. Neither scientific formulations nor philosophical categories can totally exhaust life's meaning. Ty Inbody, in "Bernard Meland, A Rebel Among Process Theologians," comments:

> Meland applies the principle of limitation explicitly to his understanding of language. Language is a fallible form. Language is not reality. Reality is the depth and complexity of the lived situation. Very early in his second period of writing he began to emphasize this point. All language is suggestive of reality rather than descriptive.[110]

Science in its quest for manageable data simplifies and abstracts from the total context of experience. The laboratory experiment becomes the operative model. Philosophy aims to be more inclusive, but rationality with its attempt to classify all experience misses the nuances and feeling tone of lived experience. Meland does not mean to dismiss either science or philosophy. Science is an aid in understanding much of our world and philosophy can be a very helpful analogy, aiding us in our attempts to investigate and probe the meaning of human experience. Even while he accepts philosophy as an aid in our quest to understand the meaning of life, he emphasizes that philosophy can point to the ultimate meanings but it cannot be a literal reading of the ultimate.[111] In this light, Meland comments on Whitehead's famous statement that "God is not an exception to the basic metaphysical principles."[112] This statement means "that insofar as one attempts to speak of God philosophically within the human framework, he must be faithful to the limitations which that framework imposes."[113] Meland is vehement in his insistence that when the philosopher or theologian thinks of principles as more than analogical, such a one has over-reached human limits. To say that God exemplifies certain

principles means that from the viewpoint of human limitation, God is seen to
exemplify these principles. The distinction between image and reality cannot
be erased. The real is always greater than and more multi-dimensioned than
any one person or system can grasp. The understanding of any individual or
system is always relative to a particular locus in history. The perspective is
always limited and even philosophy shares in this limitation.[114]

Meland is not pleading for a nonintellectual approach to matters of
philosophical and cultural importance. His vocation, after all, has been college
and university teaching. His mystical stance is not an excuse for neglecting
his academic homework. It is not an excuse for failing to use his mind, to be
as logical and clear as possible. In fact, he sees the theologian's task as a
never-ending quest for definition and clarity. Human beings need all the
clarity and intellectual rigor they possess in order to deal with the experienced
realities of existence.[115] He still insists, however, that

> since we live more deeply than we can think, no formulation of
> truth out of the language we use can be adequate for expressing
> what is really real, fully available, fully experienced within this
> mystery of existing, in the mystery of dying, or in whatever
> surpassed these creatural occurrences of such urgent moment to
> each of us.[116]

The stress in on a healthy humility in our assessment of human powers and
capabilities. Humanity never escapes its creaturehood. At one's best the
individual is always a finite being. This being so, human beings should be
alert to the danger of assuming that a particular language about reality constitutes that reality. In an article dealing with the ambiguity of the human
situation, "Grace, A Dimension within Nature," published in 1974, Meland
says,

> People differ in their responses to ambiguity. Getting clear about
> something seems to some the most important objective in life.

And of course it is in confronting certain demands and decisions. But in probing the depth of realities that form our very lives and speak to elemental depths of our creaturehood, or of our meanings as human beings, can we hope to move swiftly or even confidently simply by sharpening our tools of thought? Language itself is fallible insofar as it must employ forms and symbols fashioned out of our own limited human natures.[117]

It is this lack of humility regarding the limits of human reason that has called forth Meland's sharpest criticism of others within the empirical movement. For rationalists like Hartshorne, once a system is rationally coherent and cannot be falsified by experience, and apparently covers all known experience, it can be considered true in a very literal sense. Perceptual and conceptual relativity are downplayed. The correspondence between God's reason and human reason is thought to be great. Meland, on the other hand, sees great philosophical systems as important, semi-poetic attempts to grasp the meaning of the real, but these systems are always limited by the historical and finite minds of the individuals who produce them.

In spite of his criticism of the rational literalists, Meland does underscore the importance of the philosophical task. The philosopher's quest is an extremely important and necessary exercise for the human spirit. The philosopher serves the logos in an attempt to clarify the mythos at the base of human cultural experience.[118] It is philosophy that helps to focus humanity's attention on important matters, shaping the perceptual flux into manageable blocks of material. Philosophy helps give definiteness and to sharpen our awareness of the structures of meaning that emerge within experience. The term mythos points to the depth dimension of existence which defies complete conceptualization. The term logos points to the structure of meaning that it is possible to find within the experienced flux. Both dimensions of experience are important. The logos attempts to clarify the structures of meaning inherent in the mythos even while acknowledging that much of the meaning defies precise definition.[119]

Meland's Constructive Position

1.   Theistic Naturalism

Meland's understanding of God was developed in three clearly marked stages. In the first stage, God was viewed as a projection of human ideals. In the second stage, following Wieman's lead, God was seen as a reality separate from creation. In the third stage, Meland viewed God as a "centered other" or person. Meland wrestles with the problem of how to think about God, and concerns himself with the resources out of which a theology and a doctrine of God can be built. His doctrine of the "appreciative consciousness" is his statement of how the resources of theology should be addressed. Then on the basis of his re-assessment of the resources and methods for understanding these resources, he provides us with a theology of "reconstructed immanence."

In the first period, ending with *Modern Man's Worship* and *American Philosophies of Religion*, Meland, although using insights from James, Bergson and the Whitehead of *Religion in the Making* and the emergent philosophers, was still very close theologically to the early Chicago School. Following insights garnered from Gerald Birney Smith, he tried to show how nature itself made a theistic interpretation possible. His notion of God, however, made God either the sum of positive influences in the universe or an idealized portion of the universe. During this period Meland characterized God as empirically many, *i.e.*, empirically or functionally God is "a multiplicity of functions."[120] Only in worship are all these multiplicities synthesized into an objective oneness. In "Toward a Valid View of God," he says,

> In the hour of worship, the worshiping mind will synthesize that multiplicity into an experienced Oneness, for it is the nature of the religious mood to catch up the many into a visualized object of worship. But that describes the method of religious worship, not the condition of empirical phenomena. It is the worshiper who unifies the many to visualize the abundance of life's fullness in its totality.[121]

In that same article, he responds favorably to Ames suggestion that God is idealized reality. God is "that selective portion of the world's life, which idealized, is God."[122] This idealized portion of the universe is not what is empirically given. Even to ascribe personality to God is to assume a oneness or unity in God that is not justified by the empirical situation. Meland draws on the emergent evolutionists at this point in his argument, pointing out that human personality is one type of behavior having certain characteristics, whereas God is a certain behavior in the universe having its own functions and characteristics. God is not a person if one means by that that God is like human beings.[123] Later we will see how Meland modifies his view, though even in his latest works he wants to preserve the distinction between human persons and God as person. Whatever else God may be, God is that mystery which goes beyond human comprehension.

It was during and after working with Wieman on *American Philosophies of Religion* that Meland grew more and more disenchanted with the idea of learning more about God on the basis of objective scientific or empirical data. He did not repudiate his basic naturalism in favor of supernaturalism, but he sought a method that would probe more effectively what William James had called the "More" in experience and which Meland himself was to characterize as the depth or ultimate dimension of experience and culture. He wanted a method that would focus on the emotional and aesthetic dimensions of existence as well as on the moral and practical. In fact, Meland saw worship as debased if it were pursued for the pragmatic goal of promoting more satisfying or successful living. "Worship designed to cultivate attitudes or to develop character traits may be formative, but it can never be creative."[124] Worship that has pragmatic goals in view is basically subjective and sentimental while worship to be really aesthetic and creative needs to focus on that which is objective. He refers to Whitehead's notion that the aesthetic is more inclusive than the moral or practical.

> As Whitehead has said, the world in its deepest aspect is aesthetic, so worship in its deepest and most inclusive aspects is aesthetic, when the worshiper is alive to the impact of a great objective stirring that claims him, that evokes in him wonder, that thrills him with a sense of mystery and a sense of belonging, a sense of dependence and a feeling of commitment.[125]

2.   Resources for Theology

Meland became increasingly aware of the need for theologians in their attempts to interpret life to be as attentive to the resources of art and poetry as they were to the sciences and logic. Thus he sought to formulate a theological method that differed from the narrow and functional method of science.[126] In the preface to *The Reawakening of Christian Faith*, he speaks of the limitations of a scientific world view.

> Empiricism, by which one means, the view of the world reported by observation and experience, has become plausible to our minds, and controlling in thought. Yet, when we have pressed observation to these farthest limits, we are made aware of a *stop* in our existence; a horizon that blocks our view of things. This sense of a *stop* in life is made peculiarly vivid whenever the

mysteries of birth and death intrude upon experience. For it is then that we realize how much we live by these observations which extend our view only to the horizon. Then we are led to say that the scientific view of life is the interim view of life. Being based on observation, it is a view shorn of mystery, of mystery that extends beyond the range of observation.[127]

It was his awareness of this dimension of mystery in human existence that made him reject the scientific method as illuminative of all of human experience. "Sheer fact cannot illumine our existence."[128] This was the heresy he was spouting in a world that continued to believe that through more and more exact observation and planning modern ills could be erased. In *Seeds of Redemption*, he sets forth a rigorous critique of science and industrialism as models for understanding the essence of human life. The scientific method has led to the notions of control and power as the greatest good to the neglect of the more sensitive aspects of existence.[129] This pervasive interest in scientific control pervaded all areas of life, in the work area, in schools, in politics, and even in human relationships. Historically he sees this becoming a prominent feature of our country's life "after 1840 when America turned its back upon contemplative interests and took to the road in search of power, in search of knowledge that is power, of political rule that is power, of friendship, love and happiness that is power."[130] For Meland the issue was "between the life of power and the life of sensibilities."[131]

What was needed as Meland saw it was closer attention to that in experience which makes the qualitative dimensions possible. He rejects irrational faith and a return to supernaturalism in favor of "a more discerning religious naturalism"[132] that will take into account not just the quantitative description of events but the qualitative elements which Meland is prompted to call spirit. This religious naturalism needs to go beyond scientific thinking that knows nothing about ultimate beginnings and endings.[133] Science's dismissal of beginnings and endings of ultimate mystery gives the human person no adequate orientation for life or death. The true imagery for understanding human existence is to see it as an island with the observable terrain marked off on all sides by mystery. Meland calls for a reconstructed empiricism that will take into account these depths within human experience.[134]

In speaking about the path humanity should take, Meland sets forth his understanding of God, an understanding that goes beyond what could be known of God on the basis of scientific investigation—on the basis of clear and distinct data. It is also an understanding that goes beyond what he had said about God ten years earlier, in "Toward a Valid View of God." The term God now refers to that which stands over against finite existence. The term God no longer stands for a human projection or idealization of a part of nature.

> There is little use talking about the gospel of the sensitive life saying, this will save us, unless we believe with all our hearts that the Nature of the Infinite God that is creative of all natures is a Sensitive Nature, dedicated to the creation of the good life, the good person, the good society in ways that describe the gentle working of growth and friendship and love and mutuality among men.[135]

Meland was very aware of how his understanding of God in *Seeds of Redemption* had changed from his earlier days. He had moved from a view of God which he explicated in *Modern Man's Worship* in which God was a term used to idealize those entities in existence that contributed to human existence, to this understanding of God as an actual force within history.[136] This was one of his major breaks with the Modernists under whom he studied. He acknowledges that he broke with them on this issue of conceptualism.

> The theology of Shailer Mathews and the philosophy of Dewey and Ames will recall this form of thinking. Conceptualism abandoned the attempt of historic thought to localize deity in any

historic process and, instead, envisaged God as a word which designated certain portions of the world's life idealized, to use Ames's words; or which gathered up the personality-producing forces of the universe into an object of commitment, to put it in Shailer Mathews' language. My own thinking followed this method in *Modern Man's Worship*, wherein God was conceived in actuality as a community of activities that sustained man in existence, while in worship these many activities were unified conceptually as an object of worship.[137]

Meland came to the conclusion that our culture's procedure in scholarship, education, industry and in human relations tended to reduce "the scope of inquiry and concern to scientific proportions."[138] In so doing our society has gone far in eliminating "from thought, from feeling, from our cultural mood, that very dimension of imagination which generates a capacity for great art as well as for great faith."[139] Meland acknowledges that in his description of God as that sensitive nature that creates us all and continues to work in the world he is drawing on sources that go beyond the exact sciences. He goes to the poet and the metaphysician. He finds both the poet and the metaphysician to be employing a language that is closer to myth than to exact scientific description. For instance, exact science is not really concerned with the question of origins because there are no exact findings that can make this a truly scientific exercise. The poet and the metaphysician, however, are interested in the question of origins, "yet it is not exact knowledge of origins that poet and metaphysician seek, but a way of apprehending the large-scale idea of creation as a continual event in the life-process that contains us."[140] Both the poet and the metaphysician attempt to understand the life-process as a continuing creative event. The poet gives us penetrating glimpses of the meaning of this life-process. The metaphysician gives a comprehensive vision of the meaning of this life-process. Meland attempts to follow the insights of the poet of Genesis who sees God at work shaping the world coupled with the notions of creativity and concretion supplied by Whitehead. For both the poet of Genesis and the modern metaphysician, God is radically immanent, a God who works within history. At least this is the meaning that Meland draws from these works.

3.   The Appreciative Consciousness

Meland's puzzling over how the theologian is to get at meaning or truth within human experience led him to the methodology which he set forth at great length in 1953 in *Higher Education and the Human Spirit*. The methodology spelled out in this book coupled with his deepened understanding of the nature of God in *Seeds of Redemption* provide the basic orientation that is refined and enlarged upon in his later works. There were two methodologies current at the University of Chicago when Meland began his quest for a method that would aid the theologian in his attempt to get at the ultimate meaning in experience. The first method was that of Dewey. Like the sciences after which it was patterned, Dewey's method was functional and instrumental. The intellectual life is an instrument of action. Thinking experimentally is a problem solving activity directed toward interests in the social environment. Truth is that which works, *i.e.*, that which promotes the interests and harmony of humanity and society. The method is patterned after the controlled environment of a laboratory experiment allowing for the differences between what is possible within a rigidly controlled environment and the less controlled social environment. Analysis and inquiry are aimed at discovering those variables that will produce clear and distinct results. If human nature was an adaptive instrument for Dewey, Robert Hutchins saw human nature as being essentially intellect, with the core of the intellect as judgment. Judgment "requires the discipline of analysis that proceeds from clearly envisaged first principles."[141] Human thought is equated with logical argument. Once one knows the first principles one can analyze a situation and arrive at judgments that will promote wisdom and goodness.

Meland does not repudiate either the practical or the intellectual interests of Dewey and Hutchins, but he is primarily concerned with stressing the perceptive and imaginative side of human nature. He is concerned with quickening people's sensibilities so that a whole new range of meaning is opened to them, a range of meaning that Meland designates as spirit. Spirit is not something divorced from the natural, everyday world. It is "a quality of human discernment which embraces the good of the ethical, the intellectual, and the aesthetic life; yet seems to offer an additional dimension of goodness because it holds these concerns together as inseparable facets of the human spirit."[142] Contrary to the intellectual analysis that says a thing is understood when it is taken apart, or when its origins are uncovered, Meland's concern is with the relational context and with the "qualitative reference that transcends every single event."[143] This concern for the relational context, argues Meland, "clearly is a religious tendency in that it provides a perspective for thinking in which religious meaning may be discerned."[144]

Meland turns to William James at this point as a source of clues for reconceiving both the nature of human mind and the process of knowing. James was reacting against the notion of a transcendental ego and the subsequent notion of meaning as abstraction. The human spirit was not to be equated with the transcendental ego but with the concreteness of lived thought, "partaking of sensory experience and participating in practical pursuits."[145] Mind and body were not separate entities. "Mind was held to be simply body in its luminous, attentive, and cognitive moments; body, the mind released into an inner absorption with living."[146] As Meland saw it, "James was reaching toward an existential view of meaning and truth in which the deepest reaches of the bodily feelings along with the widest range of perceptive awareness were to be the living and actual resources."[147] Whereas Dewey's instrumentalism led to a positivistic view of experience in which what is real is that which is discoverable, James's orientation, which Meland calls radical empiricism, led to "a deeper probing of the meaning of existence."[148] James's probing of human existence led him to "the lines of demarcation where the human consciousness seemed to be bordering upon what was not man, of what, in fact was beyond man."[149] For James, the knowing mind is continually confronted with a good not its own. "The nature of the data to which mind and feeling are attuned partake of a different quality, pointing, so it seems, to a different order, yet not of a different order in the sense of its being utterly opaque or transcendental in meaning."[150]

In *A Pluralistic Universe* there is a passage which Meland quotes as being close to his understanding of what is disclosed in human experience. In that passage James says,

> The believer finds that the tenderer parts of his personal life are continuous with a more of the same quality which is operative in the universe outside of him and which he can keep in working touch with, and in a fashion get on board of and save himself, when all his lower being has gone to pieces in the wreck. In a word, the believer is continuous, to his own consciousness, at any rate, with a wider self from which saving experiences flow in...

> There is one side of life which would be easily explicable if (such) were true, but of which there appears no clear explanation so long as we assume either with naturalism that human consciousness is the highest consciousness there is, or with dualistic theism that there is a higher mind in the cosmos, but that it is discontinuous with our own...

> In spite of rationalism's disdain for the particular, the personal, and the unwholesome, the drift of all the evidence we have seems

> to me to sweep us very strongly towards the belief in some form
> of superhuman life with which we may, unknown to ourselves, be
> co-conscious. We may be in the universe as dogs and cats are in
> our libraries, seeing the books and hearing the conversation, but
> having no inkling of the meaning of it all.[151]

Meland translates this understanding into the language of the emergent evolutionists whom he sees in many ways as the heirs of James's understanding
when he says that human mind and feeling "partake of a level of spirit as
differentiated in quality and contextual organization from those representative
features of human consciousness as personality is differentiated from the
psychic structures with which it has affinities, but which it clearly
transcends."[152]

Because the object or datum which the theologian attempts to explore
and explain differs from the object of either experimental science or intellectual analysis, Meland provides us with a theological method suitable to it.
This appreciative consciousness is not a faculty of the mind or a mental
structure. It is an orientation of the total human person to the nexus of
relationships that provide both the datum and the context of the datum.
Meland agreed with James that "mind was not some one thing among many
in the organism which might be designated in the brain or in some portion of
the brain, but the whole organism seen as a psychical body, dormant at times,
but at any instant ready to be roused into action as conscious awareness."[153] It
is an attempt to be aware of the intuitions of experience that provide the
background of our clear, conscious knowledge. Whereas both science and
academic disciplines engage in analysis and are intent on abstracting a clear
datum from the perceptual flux, the appreciative consciousness "can best be
understood as an orientation of the mind which makes for a maximum degree
of receptivity to the datum under consideration on the principle that what is

given may be more than what is immediately perceived, or more than one can think."[154]

Further, it should be noted that the appreciative consciousness does not attempt to exhaust the meaning of the datum with preconceived premises or categories. The appreciative consciousness attempts to perceive the raw texture of lived experience. The appreciative consciousness tries to be open to the fact that "what is given in any object stands in a context of mystery which always defies precise formulation."[155] What one perceives always points beyond itself. The actual event points towards its future (the possible) but also to hidden aspects of its present existence. "Whether one is speaking of some happening, a person, an institution, the living community, or of God, one is dealing with an inexhaustible event, the fullness of which bursts every defini- tive category."[156] When the appreciative consciousness is operative "a sense of the-more-than-the-mind can grasp as well as a sense of expectancy concerning every event, knowing that creativity is occurring, that time is real, attends every act of cognition."[157] The appreciative consciousness is the human person oriented toward every relation either perceived or imagined that forms the context of the object.

Through this methodology, Meland hopes to stay true to the naturalistic theological school out of which he came and at the same time do justice to elements of human experience that are missed by scientific inquiry and philosophical analysis. Two important themes which Meland returns to again and again in his writings correspond to his methodology. The first theme is that the individual is a finite being who cannot grasp the structure of the real with only the conscious intellect. The second theme is that the "more" that impinges on human limits can be perceived if not comprehended by the conscious intellect. By considering the "more" that goes beyond conscious formulations, the appreciative consciousness is "subjectively enriched by the intrusion of novel relations into its stream of previously structured experience."[158] The appreciative consciousness is a stance of openness to the depths and nuances of experience that go beyond cognitive formulations and which cannot be expressed in pragmatic-functional terms. It is an openness towards other people, other cultures, towards the natural environment and toward "the God who is creative of us all,"[159] the God who Meland calls "a Sensitive Nature within Nature."[160]

The appreciative consciousness is that orientation toward human experience and human cultures that tries to get at that which is ultimate. As J. Gerald Janzen has pointed out in an intriguing article entitled "Meland as Yahwistic Theologian of Culture," Meland's approach to theologizing is very similar to that of the Old Testament historians. For both, this modern theologian and his ancient predecessors, determined the presence of God by looking at historical, human experience. Though separated by many centuries, they both attempt to trace out and give witness to the work of the divine within history.[161] It is the appreciative consciousness that has enabled Meland to produce a theology of radical immanence. Unlike the classic mystic who attempts to flee from concrete historical existence into some trans-ethereal sphere Meland, as a mystical naturalist, seeks to plumb the depths of concrete existence in order to find the God who is at work within history, shaping the world and the cultures within which human beings live. Meland is similar to the classic mystic, however, in his affirmation that the reality encountered goes beyond cognitive expression. It is from this perspective that he comments favorably on the work of William James:

> James' evident respect for what he called "the perceptual flux," as conveying much in experience *as lived* that could not be conceptualized, led him to acknowledge its primacy as the empirical datum, and to recoil from overzealous efforts to cast its meaning

in conceptual terms, or to presume to envisage it imaginatively or abstractly through rational explications.[162]

4.   Reconstructed Immanence

In this section we will concern ourselves with Meland's mature theological statement. The three most important works in this period are *Faith and Culture*, *Realities of Faith*, and *Fallible Forms and Symbols*. Using the insights and methodology garnered from his earlier phases Meland turned his attention to understanding in greater detail the problem of the relation between Christian faith and culture and the limitations of language when matters of ultimate importance are discussed. Basic to Meland's constructive position, which he sees as not a rejection of the spirit of the liberalism of an earlier age but as a reconstruction, is the differences between the resources from which they work. Both the older liberals and Meland see themselves as working within the limits of modern science and philosophy. However, "the earlier, historic liberalism was basically neo-Kantian in its philosophical method and perspective, Darwinian or Spencerian in its view of evolution, and Newtonian in its understanding of the fundamental notions relating to the physical universe."[163] This was as true according to Meland for the American pragmatists as it was for those such as the Ritschlians, Hegelians, Personalists and Positivists who more clearly show their European roots. In all these groups within the contemporary scene, Kant's "dissociation of the subjective ego from the context of objective relations persisted with remarkable tenacity, causing the human dimension of consciousness to be regarded as the source and center of spiritual meaning and value."[164] This humanistic bias was reinforced by the liberals' understanding of Darwin and Spencer as meaning that the human species was the height of creation.

The new liberalism draws on James, Bergson, and Whitehead, rather than Kant and Hegel in philosophy. It looks to the works of the emergent evolutionists such as Lloyd Morgan and Jan Smuts instead of Darwin and Spencer, and finally the new physics replaces the old Newtonian, mechanistic world view. Philosophically, this means that human essence can no longer be conceived as ego divorced from concrete relations. This relational context also means that a people's faith cannot be discerned by simply analyzing a set of intellectual beliefs. Faith is a more basic part of the human situation than that. As he says in reference to faith, "It is the formative ground of man's valuations, reaching the inmost parts of the human psyche, where the meaning of the person or personality and the sense of meaning relating the person to the wider life about him is subtly fashioned."[165]

From James, Bergson, and Whitehead, Meland learned to take seriously the relational context. From the emergent evolutionists with their notion of distinct levels of emergence, he learned to think of human beings as distinctive in their own right and not to confuse them or their consciousness with that which supersedes humanity.

> In the works of the emergent evolutionists, man as distinctly man appears vividly. The distinguishing features of the human creation stand out in their own right. Likewise, the limiting factors of the human consciousness which sets man clearly apart from what is more than man, and which impels man not to think more highly of himself than he ought to think, are made vivid by this understanding of human emergence.[166]

Meland also looked to anthropology for insights that would become part of his mature theology. He draws on insights of myth-making and myth-consciousness derived from the modern science of anthropology. Myth speaks to the total relational context of a people, revealing the valuations that lie at the core of their culture. "Myth-making and myth-consciousness" reveal "the nature of the feeling context of the race in which sensibilities have emerged and in which the controlling valuations of the culture have taken form."[167] They suggest the way in which faith can be understood "as a cultural resource and as a social energy."[168]

Faith has two dimensions.

> Faith in its immanent aspect is the condition of trust which comes to dominate the psychical experiences of a people or a person, preparing them to confront the ultimate mystery of existence; or simply to find innumerable instances which awaken man to his limits, his creaturehood, and his dependence.[169]

Faith in its transcendent dimension is a gift of grace. It is a gift of grace that assures us that we are related to other creatures and ultimately to God, the ground of our being. Faith in its transcendent dimension, faith as a gift of grace, is recognized as a goodness that transcends both human experience and culture. Faith is a gift of grace witnessing to a goodness that is other than one's own.

> Faith, as this transcendent condition of trust reclaiming us, issues forth out of the matrix of sensitivity that is in the life of God expressing itself through the communal ground, evoking a recon- ception of experience and culture and of the primordial condition of trust as well.[170]

Faith as an immanent aspect is given to humanity in Creation. Faith as transcendent has its source in the redemptive act. It should be noted that Meland uses transcendent to refer to that which is within the historical-tem- poral sphere and not to delineate something beyond or outside of this sphere.

Since Meland defines faith as basically an attitude of trust and as an assurance that is given, faith can never adequately be defined as assent to creeds or theological statements. He finds that within the history of Western culture whenever faith has been identified with objective statements about the faith, it has served to repress or suppress the living element within the faith.[171] This does not mean that persons individually or in community should give up the search for definition and clarity. It does mean that the attempt to define what trust means is a never ending task for each generation.

While denying that any formulation is adequate to express faith, Meland joins the pietists of an earlier generation in assuming that faith is an assurance, it is not a gamble in the face of a lack of evidence. Within the Christian community,

> the earliest records of the witnessing community express not so much a venture of trust against possible odds as an assurance of grace given in the act of Revelation to which the witness is borne.[172]

The witnessing community formulated their trust in kerygma or in a body of doctrine; thus trust always implies a content of meaning. For Meland, the content is that the ultimate condition of our existence is "that our life is in God."[173] Meland's formulation as the earlier formulations is not a final statement about "trust." Experienced reality always goes beyond the limitations of language and no formulation of the basic experience ever has the authority of that experience.

a.   Myth, Mythos and Culture

The basic intuitions that faith provides is what Meland terms myth. Myth is the basic ingredient in both mythology and mythos. It is through myth, mythology and mythos that culture mediates the "more" that appears in human experience. By addressing himself to myth, mythology, and mythos, Meland intends to attempt to unpack the meaning of ultimate reality as it is mediated to us in Western culture and in human experience. Myth is the most basic term and it refers to "the human response to actuality in its ultimate dimension."[174] Myth is similar to Bergson's "intuition." Myth makes us sensitive to the limits of conscious human intellect and aware of the discontinuities within the stream of human experience. It is a sensitivity to that which lies beyond our comprehension. For Meland,

> Myth reaches to the level of the creaturely stance which a people will assume in speaking of their existence. It affects and shapes, not only language, the mode of thinking and speaking, but sensibilities of thought, psychical orientation, thus psychical expectations. One senses this as one moves from one orbit of cultural meaning to another. Different myths have insinuated into the very historical heritage of the respective cultures a continuing fabric of meaning which has immediate and intrinsic intelligibility within that cultural orbit. It directs the way human beings normally think and feel, as one might say; but one really means it is the way human beings normally think within that historic orbit of existence.[175]

Meland sees the Christian myth as formative of Western culture in the same way as the myth of Karma and transmigration of the later Vedas gives meaning to traditions and social mores in India. Even when you consider the revolt of much of European intelligentsia against the Christian faith and the official position of separation of church and state in America, "the fact remains that the Christian myth, as a cultural force, whether approved or rejected, has continued through all these centuries to give a certain character, a certain pattern, to the emotional and cognitive life of Europe and America."[176] Myth does not give "definitive meaning to any reality, experience or event;"[177] the function of myth is to keep experience alive to the ultimate reality that lies beyond the borders of one's finite existence. The Christian myth affirms God's creative activity, human creaturehood, and the covenental relationship between humanity and God. Meland draws on Whitehead's notion of *causal efficacy* to illuminate the way in which the Christian faith has influenced Western culture. *Causal efficacy* is the doctrine that all meanings that have emerged in the space-time continuum are prehended by each successive emergent event and thus these meanings persist in some form and in some degree to give character to each succeeding event. "The Christian myth as a unitary organization of seminal ideas, the origin of which we are in no position to clarify, remains the source of the formative insights of our Western culture in ways that compare with the impress of family traits upon the protoplasm."[178]

Myth or the mythical attitude is not something that can be eliminated or translated into any other idiom, even the idiom of existentialism. Thus Meland views the attempt at de-mythologizing by Brunner and his school as at best a mis-guided and wrong-headed approach. Myth cannot be disposed of by anyone wishing to be attentive to that dimension of existence that stands over against us and makes us aware of our creaturehood.[179] Myth preserves the gap between what is rationally manageable and what is unmanageable in human experience. To suggest, as Schubert Ogden does, that myth can be understood as analogy is likewise misleading if one then proceeds to turn that analogy into rational metaphysical categories.[180] Myth is as important for modern people as it was for people of earlier ages. Again, quoting from Meland's own words helps to clarify his argument.

> My concern with myth has been motivated, in fact, by the realization that analogy as employed in metaphysics appears unable to hold back the floodwaters of rationalism, once the tenuous "appeal for an imaginative leap" gives way to a more definitive mood of logical analysis. This may be because analogy stresses the note of continuity between thought and being, and does not stress sufficiently the discontinuity that exists. Myth, on the other hand, at

least registers the shock of disparity between my thoughts as a
human formulation and the reality that is other than my thoughts.
I admit it is a weasel word, as Schubert Ogden's discussion in
Christ Without Myth continually implies. Nevertheless, I would
argue that we cannot dispose of it, in so far as we choose to be
attentive to that dimension of existence which elicits our sense of
creaturehood.[181]

As Meland sees it, not even Bultmann can really dispose of myth.

When I observe a meticulous and highly sensitive scholar like
Bultmann proceeding with his method of demythologizing to
interpret Christian faith exhaustively and without remainder as
man's original possibility of authentic historical existence, and
then making, as it were, a sharp turn from this procedure in his
appeal to the saving event of Jesus Christ, by way of preserving
the Kerygma, something demonic in me leaps with glee, and I
want to shout for joy.[182]

Bultmann's refusal to go all the way with his demythologizing indicates to
Meland that it is impossible to do away with the primacy of reality over
reason. Reality always goes beyond that which can be put into a logical or
rational structure, and human response to that reality must contain elements of
metaphor and analogy and thus partakes of mythical discourse. Human limitation makes the language of myth a necessity.

The metaphorical response to the saving act of God in history,
that subtle and complex instance of attending to ultimacy in our
immediacies, to the mystery of the Kingdom in the midst of
historical circumstances, is thus seen to be a persisting and
unexpendable witness to the very realities that inform and sustain
our authentic existence.[183]

Though myth is a non-expendable element in culture, Meland is willing
to admit that mythologies understood as "objectifying the powers of Spirit into
a supernaturalism, a super-history transcending or supervening our human
history, thus forming a *double history*"[184] can be altered. Like all attempts of

human language to express the ultimate dimension of existence, mythologies are fallible and inadequate, always standing under the judgement of the realities in experience to which they refer. In so far as all that Bultmann means by myth is mythologies, Meland admits he has a point. These mythologies can be expanded, retold and even in some cases eliminated, but Bultmann is wrong even here when he suggests that the initial truth which mythologies grasp can be simply translated into rational or existential terms. Myth, upon which mythologies build, is a deeper orientation in a culture than a mere cognitive notion. Furthermore, myth is a pervasive influence throughout an entire culture. Thus to suggest, as Bultmann does in Kerygma and Myth that "Heidegger's existentialist analysis of the ontological structure of being would seem to be no more than a secularized, philosophical version of the New Testament view of human life,"[185] and to further state that "that philosophy is saying the same thing as the New Testament and saying it quite independently,"[186] is to overlook the pervasive influence of the Christian story in Western culture. In a somewhat ironical tone, Meland suggests that to speak of a philosopher as independently arriving at truth also found within the New Testament is to

> overlook the fact that all thought occurs within a cultural matrix. Once the revelation of God in Jesus Christ became a concrete historical fact of Western experience, there was no concealing it, not even from philosophers. Or to state it differently, no thinking or feeling of man's being within its orbit of meaning and experience was immune from its shaping. A philosopher may not say, "Jesus Christ is Lord." He may not even acknowledge the name, or think of it. He will still feed upon the sensibilities of thought that issue from its nurturing matrix. Thus to say that a philosopher, even when he is Heidegger, all by himself sees what the New Testament says, is to appear to have no sense of historical context; certainly not the kind of contextual sensitivity which the cultural anthropologist has come to understand and value.[187]

Meland uses the term mythos as a broader term than either myth or mythology. In *Faith and Culture*, mythos refers to "the pattern of meaning and valuations which has been imaginatively projected through drama or metaphor, expressing the historic truths of the historic experience of a people, bearing upon man's nature and destiny."[188] In *Fallible Forms and Symbols*, these words are added to the basic definition,

> as these perceptive truths of experience express themselves within the culture as psychic energy in the form of hopes, expectations, attitudes of trust or apprehension, or even determination; or in the human response to circumstances joyous or tragic, promising or threatening, and similar historical occurrences affecting the stance in meeting human situations.[189]

Mythos includes the basic intuitions (myth), the mythologies and all the artistic and symbolic ways in which these have penetrated Western culture. The images which are drawn from the seminal insights of the Christian faith do not have to be explicitly Christian in order for them to reflect the basic pattern of meaning and valuations traceable to the Christian myth.

Earlier in *The Reawakening of Christian Faith*, Meland had set forth the basic valuations that he sees arising from the Christian myth. This myth begins with the Creation in Genesis, sin and consequent sorrow, the New Creation in Jesus Christ, the crucifixion and resurrection and its subsequent redemptive influence on man. The first valuation is that life is good. Life is "the structures created by the Creator for the attainment of spirit in His image."[190] The second valuation is "that individual life is sacred and meaningful in the drama of creation."[191] The third valuation is that every created individual expects to realize fulfillment. The fourth valuation is "that human fulfillment is not linear, not the mere process of self-realization, for man's powers are impaired by the fact of his individuality which sets him at tension, both with his Creator and with the community of all creatures."[192] The final valuation is that individual fulfillment comes through sacrificial love rather than through self-love. "The sheer clinging to the concerns of one's individual existence, untempered by sacrificial love, retards, rather than advances, one's fulfillment," is the way Meland puts the matter.[193] These valuations as they are worked out in diverse and complex ways in culture constitute the mythos of our culture.

The importance of the individual is underlined in these valuations of Meland's, and in "From Darwin to Whitehead" Meland again notes the importance of the individual for religion. For him it is not a correct understanding of relational thought to assume that the individual is subsumed into community. "The truer imagery is the one formulated by Whitehead, in saying that the topic of religion is individual in community, which is to see individual values empowered through relationships, and the community expressive of freedom and qualitative differences."[194] Again in "New Dimensions of Liberal Faith," Meland emphasizes the prime significance of the individual. "The insight of liberalism that the self-experience of individual man is of infinite worth before God, even when it conflicts with the divine intention, is a restoration of the most discerning and precious heritage of the Hebraic-Christian faith."[195] The Christian theologians task, as Meland sees it, is to be attentive to the ways in which the importance of the individual and the other valuations are incorporated into a patterned mythos which persists in Western culture. For Meland, response to the ultimate always takes place within a particular cultural matrix. This is the reason he looks askance at any theology or theologian that pretends that Christianity (or any other religion) is a non-culturally conditioned religion.[196] As a corollary to this, he rejects the notion that any theology can deal with God as deity existing within itself or as God existing beyond the historical-temporal sphere.[197] The basic mythos of a culture, with which theology deals, arises out of a people's wrestling with the ultimate depth within experience. The perceptive truths arising out of this grasp of the ultimate within its midst are embodied in a people's mythos, and this mythos helps shape the culture from that point onward.

We may get a better grasp of what Meland is doing if we contrast his orientation with the stance of the radical Barthians and with Tillich. Unlike the Barthians, Meland does not assume that the Christian message is something totally divorced from culture, for Western culture itself, is at least partly a child of the basic confrontation with the ultimate that gets imaginative treatment in the Christian mythos. Once the mythos is formulated, it continues to shape and influence culture. For this reason, Meland rejects Tillich's assumption that culture is the locus of questions to which the Christian faith gives answers. It is almost asking the chicken and egg question to ask which comes first—the mythos or the culture. The historical experience of a people arising out of its wrestling with "what is ultimate in the reality of things"[198] gets embodied in its mythos and that mythos continues to shape and influence culture. The experience of a people in a given historical context produces the mythos and the mythos influences the culture—culture generates the mythos and mythos generates the culture. The relation is always subtle and complex. Both the questions and answers within a given cultural matrix are shaped by the mythos.

Thus there is a sense in which Meland's theology cannot adequately be described as a theology of culture.[199] He is not attempting to show that the values of a given culture are divine. His attempt is to trace the workings of God within a given culture as those workings are delineated within a given mythos. Meland assumes that "the immediacies of concrete experience actually participate in the depth of the Creative Passage in which the human structure of sensory life is integrally related to other structures, and to what is genuinely ultimate as a dynamic of creativity."[200] For Meland, God is at work in the depths of all human experience; therefore he does not focus on special religious experience or on the experiences of rare individuals. Theoretically, God's grace is available to all people, limited only by an individual's failure to accept or be open to the workings of grace in life.

> Grace is always a gift of the goodness that waits to be apprehended in any situation to soften the sting of evil or loss, and to reassure the broken or defeated spirit of man. Whether or not grace has actuality in an individual's existence will depend upon how ready he is to receive the good that awaits him in each such situation. Every moment is a creative situation in which lethargy, evil, and the good that is of God's working, contrive to be sovereign.[201]

It is the work of God within the structure of experience which produces any qualitative emergence. The ultimate source of all experienced good is God. This grace that meets us in human experience as part of the structure of experience is ultimately given by God. All individuals have access to this grace which is given, "but the sensitive working of God is never adequately known by any one of us."[202] Whatever results from the working of God within the structures of human experience is always a complex of God's work and humanity's work so "that no easy contrasting of God and culture is possible."[203] Individuals can thwart the urgings of God to develop greater sensitivity and spiritual qualities but can also cooperate with God in order to bring about a new and creative advance.

Meland assumes that the basic insights that are embodied in myth and which get translated into poetry, song and drama always point to a "deeper, less articulate, emotional context."[204] This feeling context, Meland designates as "structure of experience."[205] This structure is an elemental awareness that does not have definite cognitive meaning. Feeling context is probably a better word for that which Meland intends to describe. While all events enter into this feeling context in some manner or other, the feeling context is not simply the accumulation of all events. Its qualitative character arises out of that which is rejected or minimized and that which is retained. What is retained is not simply of a positive character, but both positive and negative events become molded and transformed in the feeling context. All individuals exist in this feeling context that is beyond their own making, but individuals are not therefore bound to simply automatically repeat the feeling context. For each individual has the potentiality for creativity and can and probably does introduce novelty into the emerging structure. "Nevertheless, all living persons carry within their conscious existence and in their perceptual nature something of the hidden drives and aspirations which rise out of this accumulative structure of experience."[206] At the deepest recesses of experience, God is at work transforming sheer process into qualitative attainment. The Christian myth seeks to bear witness to the God who is working to create out of the brute facts of history qualitative good. Within Western culture Christ becomes the focal point for this feeling context.

> It is the testimony of our culture at its deepest level that the basic
> event of our history, giving witness to this perception of good as
> sovereign for all existence, is the person, Jesus Christ. This is the
> implication of the myth; it is also the accepted judgment of
> metaphysics whenever it seeks to give cognitive explanation of
> the *tenderness of life* to which the myth bears witness.[207]

For Meland, the hopes and aspirations articulated by the prophets, the betrayals and destructive energy are all transformed or redeemed in this historical event, Jesus Christ. Something creative and novel has arisen in history that accepts the failures and rebellions as well as the qualitative insights of the past and transmutes them into a new synthesis of creativity within our culture. This New Creation is not divorced from the past nor is it simply a repetition of the past but introduces new sensitivity and meaning into every subsequent happening. Christian faith is the affirmation of "this formative myth that bears witness to the creative good of existence."[208]

Faith is not assent to creeds or to precise formulations. Meland says,

> Faith is the fruition of an age-long venture of dedication and inquiry among any people in response to a persisting concern about their cultural destiny. More than a set of beliefs, the faith is a set of the mind and an orientation of the human psyche which have emerged within the structure of experience of the Western culture, availing man of resources that are deeper and more enduring than his own creations, for they arise from the creative source of life itself: the work of God in history.[209]

Simply stated, the picture Meland presents is this. God originates the process and continues to work within creation. The working of God in conjunction with the cooperation or rejection of humankind makes up the feeling context or structure of experience that provides the basic intuitions that are perceived in myth. Faith affirms the basic mythic intuitions that are expressed in the Christian mythos.

Through his analysis of the structures of experience as they are revealed in the mythos of a culture, Meland attempts to provide a fuller picture of the working of God than can be found within the written scriptures, creeds, theologies, and worship taken by themselves. This analysis of culture does not take the place of nor supersede the importance of the others but is conceived by Meland as an adjunct and aid to understanding. Through his analysis of culture and specifically his analysis of the Christian mythos, Meland hopes to come to terms with God, "this gentle working that creates friendship, community, love, and the beauty of wholeness among nature."[210] Through his analysis he hopes to come to terms with "the enduring creativity that can shape our course toward peace, overcoming hatred, bigotry, and suffering and ultimately triumphing over the tragic sense of life itself."[211]

Meland's concern to give witness to the uniqueness of that which is ultimate in human existence makes him very careful about preserving the distinction between God and finite humanity. As noted earlier, Meland initially rejected the notion of God as personal, because he thought it led to the fallacy that God was simply human existence writ large. Although we shall later see that he modified his strictures against using person in relation to God, he still is very careful to speak of God as a different level of emergence than finite humanity, or as that which stands over against humanity, the more that meets humanity at the edge of conscious experience. Meland's stress on the otherness of God unites him with the Continental theologians though his and their constructive positions are far apart. Meland is concerned with that otherness that meets us in the immediacies of our present existence. Thus he calls his theology a theology of immanence.

> Immanence simply presupposes that there are structures within the reach and recognition of man which disclose God's working in some form and to some degree. This does not deny the hiddenness of God. In fact, in reconstructed form it heartily affirms it as a corollary of God's recognizable aspect. This principle of correlating the clearly given and the obscure occurrent will be seen to be indispensable to a reconstructed liberalism.[212]

b.   Mythos and Logos

Meland's insistence on the fact of God's otherness leads him to deny that any one structure within human existence can be the link between humanity and God. This is the basis of his critical evaluation of all liberal theology since the enlightenment. Liberal theologians tended to see human consciousness as the link between humanity and God. In so doing they tended to narrow the sources of religious inquiry and thus not to do justice to the full scope of God's working within history. Schleiermacher, for example, "by specifying the religious consciousness as the normative source of doctrine ...excluded a whole range of theological inquiries which might press the mind into speculative ventures."[213] Human consciousness, for Schleiermacher and those who were his heirs, was the criterion by which all things, even God, were to be judged. The end result for the liberal era was that God became a creation of the human consciousness; a God fashioned in the likeness of humanity. This led to a deficiency both in the understanding of humanity and of the understanding of God. Humanity was no longer conceived as having a depth of being and God loses the element of mystery. Both of these elements are crucial for Meland's thought. When human consciousness becomes the pinnacle of creation and the norm for judging all of creation, "this removes the depth of being not only from man but from God as well. The mystery of God's being vanishes or becomes unimportant."[214]

Meland's cultural analysis seeks to retain the liberal doctrine of immanence but at the same time to get beyond the simple reductionism of traditional liberalism. By drawing on the insights of emergent thinkers, he attempts to provide a reconstructed immanence. This reconstructured immanence implies "structural limitations at all levels of life, thereby precluding any simple projection of the description of the human mind or personality to a depiction of ultimate reality, or the character of the mind of God."[215] Meland's analysis of culture attempts to hold in tension both a certain amount of clarity as we attempt to think about the primordial mythos that shapes our society and openness to the mystery that goes beyond creaturely experience. Meland calls this approach to theological problems an appeal to sanity and not to rationality.

I regard the doctrine of immanence as a crucial premise to be retained because upon its retention, to whatever degree, however altered or reconstructed, rests what I call the sanity of the theological enterprise. Notice I do not say reasonableness of the enterprise. I am parting company with rationality as an arbitrary norm or generalized feature of existence in the sense in which idealism insisted upon it. Sanity does not presuppose a completely rational order of existence. It simply implies a margin of rationality in the midst of irrational and unpredictable factors which, nevertheless, assures sufficient order and meaningfulness to enable us to function intelligibly in a context of related disciplines.[216]

In *Fallible Forms and Symbols,* Meland speaks of the relation of logos and mythos as a way of understanding the relation of rationality and mystery for theology.

Logos implies the level of rationality implicit in experience which is available through an overt inquiry into conscious experience; while mythos, on the other hand, addresses a depth of awareness which, while available to conscious experience, functions in the main as a noncognitive mode of meaning and motivation in the living structure of experience of any people or culture.[217]

Neither of the two—mythos or logos—can be translated into the idiom of the other. The logos functions to draw clarity and structure out of human experience, while the mythos functions to qualify and enrich cognitive understanding. For Meland, structure is not something that the mind adds to experience as might appear to be the case in a Kantian formulation. Form or logos is part of the experienced reality, but this form or structure can only be apprehended not comprehended. Thus he can say that intelligibility is "an occurrence of knowing that sees the intelligible focus of meaning within a context of unfocused, yet intimately associated experience."[218]

c.   Primary Document

In Western culture, the document that contains the seminal and formative insights that are basic to the mythos that has evolved is the Bible. Meland does not deny that there have been other bodies of literature venerated as sacred in the West such as the sagas of the Norsemen or the legends of the Druids or even the Greek mythologies. None of these other literatures, however, have had the pervasive and persistent influence that the scriptures have had. At least since the time of Constantine in the West, there have been two levels of witness to the importance of the Scriptures. The first is the authoritative and institutional consensus. This witness derives from the church's acceptance of this body of literature as being expressive of its own life and meaning. After the 4th century, the church was given the authorization and the power to codify the insights of this literature in political and social codes and institutions. At the same time, there was at work within culture the Word coming through the scriptures "which was persistently being rediscovered or attended to in remote centers by various communities which were to erupt into renascent piety groups."[219] The authoritative witness and the persistent witness of faith both testified to the supremacy of the Bible as a cultural influence.

The historical test of whether the Biblical mythos is seminal and formative of Western culture is derived from four criteria according to Meland. These are:

> (1) its pervasiveness; (2) its durability as a continuing witness of faith; (3) its renewability, or renascent power, in various periods of Western history; and (4) its defensibility—that is, its ability to remain consistently persuasive as true to the exigencies of the lived experience and to reflection within various perspectives that have been brought to bear on it, and within various idioms through which it has been expressed.[220]

When speaking of the influence of the Christian mythos or the influence that the Bible has had on Western culture, Meland is not speaking of the way in which the official theology or liturgy of the church has been molded. He is speaking of how the seminal strands of the formative legacy have persisted as bearers of the basic themes and motifs, however these get reshaped, within Western culture. He speaks this way out of the conviction that "faith is a deeper psychical and realistic event within the culture than this cultic experience, defined and conveyed through church doctrine and history, has made evident, and than theologians generally have recognized."[221] For Meland, faith is a more pervasive element within culture than theologians have acknowledged. "Its apprehensions and sensibilities spread wide and far throughout the social experience."[222] Much of its influence remains unarticulated and latent serving "as an overtone of common thought, or an undertow of feeling."[223] At one and the same time it affects both the articulate speech and actions of a people within a given cultural history. A people dissociates itself from these seminal insights of the past at its own peril, because these insights shape whatever qualitative attainment is possible in the present. Staying in tune with the seminal insights of the past is not simply a remembering of those events which convey those meanings. As Meland says in regards to Jesus Christ:

> I am concerned to say that responding to the revelatory event in Jesus Christ is not just a matter of perpetuating the recollection and psychical shaping of an historical event through memory and tradition, but of experiencing a work of judgment and grace concretely in the depth of present events and relationships.[224]

Theological method begins with the present moment, looking at the empirical shape of faith within a given historical context. It returns to the primal source and norm of faith in the mythos and then moves to the present to provide an intelligible witness to the faith.[225]

d.   Formative Motif

For Meland, the formative motif of the Christian mythos is the redemptive
theme. This redemptive theme was developed in folklore, prophetic sermons,
poetry and the law. It reached new heights in the life of Jesus. In Jesus, "the
reality of a new consciousness, *a new Creation*, did come into history, giving
rise to a *revelation in act*, to use Whitehead's phrase, what had been *divined
in theory*.[226] Meland does not see a simple contrast between law and gospel as
has sometimes been pointed to within Christian faith.

> The law itself had emerged out of sensitive apprehensions distilled
> from generations of living, and the gospel, for all its forbearance
> and openness to the spontaneous and innovating good, subsumed
> within its gracious acts the integrity of the law as a witness to
> the role of judgment.[227]

Redemption both for Judaism and for Christianity is expressed in the
root metaphor of covenant—the covenant relationship between finite humanity
and God.[228] As Meland understands it, in the Hebraic or Old Testament
setting, "personality was a communal term."[229] To speak of God and humanity
in this context meant that one was speaking of God and God's people. Under
the impact of the Christ-figure, this relationship was individualized. The
individual becomes the focus of the covenental relationship and the community is seen as an extension of this relationship. For the Hebrews what it
meant to be human was mediated to the individual by the community. For the
Christian, what it means to live in community is mediated by Jesus, this
individual's relation to God. The community is an outgrowth of the individual
relationship with God.[230]

The theme of redemption presupposes that there is a rift in the covenental relationship. Meland sees this not so much as suggesting that there was

something inherently wrong or evil in humanity, but as deriving "more directly from the strain implicit in the covenant relationship."[231] It is "an inescapable condition of dissonance in relationships where two or more centers of dignity are involved."[232] Dissonance always accompanies freedom and dignity, even when one of the centers is God. The encounter between God and humanity is not the encounter of slave with master but an "I-Thou" encounter.[233] Therefore in any encounter between God and humanity there is the possibility of difference. Within Christian theology this difference between humanity and God has traditionally been called sin. If human existence is to be human existence and not just an extension of God, if it is to maintain its own center then it is inescapably a sinner. To speak of finite humanity as sinner then "is to recognize frankly the limited character of the human structure simultaneously with acknowledging its authenticity as a concrete, innovating center of witness."[234]

The redemptive work of God in attempting to sustain a qualitative relationship with the limited human structure becomes thematized as the Suffering Servant. Within the New Testament the deeper import of this theme becomes explicit. There the work of Christ is rendered "as God taking on the form of a man and reconciling the world to himself."[235] Here God is depicted as taking the initiative in a gracious, redemptive act, whereby God identifies completely with sinful, suffering humanity. God is seen as having an active sensitive role within human events, trying to negotiate with finite humanity to bring about good for the individual and for the community. This good which is not humanity's own that reaches out to humanity brings a note of forgiveness for human failures, pride and refusal to acknowledge the deeper community of God and humanity of which humanity is a part. Acceptance of that forgiveness involves a "response of faithfulness in the covenant relationship."[236]

The climax of the work of the suffering servant is the resurrection. The structured meaning of this theme "is an affirming note beyond tragedy, a living forward in trust, despite the immediacies of anguish and defeat."[237] The resurrection is "a final declaration of hope in the relational ground of the covenant, namely, that our life is in God."[238] The resurrection "has given a sense of openness and expectancy transcending the closures and despairs of experience and history."[239]

e.   God

In Meland's earliest statement, as was noted above, God was seen as a projection of humanity's highest ideals. Under the influence of Wieman he came to an understanding of God's work as totally different from human work. At this early period, he used the imagery of the emergent evolutionists to stress that God's level of being is discontinuous with the lower level which is human. Under the influence of the poets and Whitehead's philosophy, he came to think of God as a sensitive working within nature. By the time he wrote *Faith and Culture*, though still rejecting the notion that God is simply continuous with any aspect of human nature, he can say,

> The imagery of parental care which the Hebraic-Christian faith has employed to convey the personal relationship between God and His creatures is sound so long as the imagery is not used to reduce God to human stature and thus to mythologize a meaning which really transcends man's mind even as it cradles and nurtures the whole of man's existence. God stands to man as one structure of meaning stands to another. This is the import of the father-son imagery.[240]

In *Fallible Forms and Symbols*, while still maintaining the mystery and otherness of God, Meland speaks of centers of dignity to describe both human existence and God. God is a center of dignity just as an individual human being is and the relationship is an "I-Thou" relationship. The notion of prehension helps to convey what Meland means at this point. "Each entity, including God, prehends every other entity with varying degrees of relevance."[241] Prehension implies that there is no simple immanence whereby an individual by looking within can find God; God is always prehended as the other at the base of human experience, available to human beings but other than human beings. "This correlation of otherness and withness"[242] is Meland's reconstructed notion of immanence. Within this reconstructed immanence God is both the Ground of our being and the Ultimate Efficacy within relationships. To use traditional theological terms, God is both creator and redeemer. God's power initiated the process and works within the process as the power that works for redemption.

1. Cf. Larry Axel, "The Root and Form of Meland's Elementalism," *Journal of Religion* 60 (October 1980): 483-484; Meland, "In Response to Miller," 114; Miller, *American Spirit in Theology*, 61; and Gerald Birney Smith, "The Nature of Science and of Religion and their Interrelation," *Religious Education* 23 (1927): 308, 310.

2. Kaplan, "The Way I have Come," 289.

3. Meland, "In Response to Miller," 109.

4. Bernard Meland, "Reflections on the Early Chicago School of Modernism," *American Journal of Theology and Philosophy* 5 (January 1984): 7.

5. Ibid.

6. Ibid., 6–7.

7. Ibid., 9.

8. Ibid., 10.

9. Ibid.

10. Ibid., 12.

11. Meland, "Empirical Tradition in Theology," 18. Cf. Bernard Meland, "Chicago School of Theology," *Encyclopedia of Religious Knowledge* (Grand Rapids: Baker Book House, 1955), vol.1, 232–233.

12. Wieman and Meland, *Philosophies of Religion*, 291.

13. Bernard Meland, "Is God Process or Person?" *The Christian Century* (January 29, 1947): 134.

14. Cf. Bernard Meland, *Higher Education and the Human Spirit* (Chicago: University of Chicago Press, 1953), 79–109.

15. Bernard Meland, "The Genius of Protestantism," *The Journal of Religion* 27 (1947): 238.

16. Ibid., 284.

168The American Empirical Movement in Theology

17. Bernard Meland, "The Appreciative Approach in Religion," *The Journal of Religion* 14 (1934): 199.

18. Ibid., 199–200.

19. Ibid., 202.

20. Bernard Meland, "Reflections on the Early Chicago School of Modernism," *American Journal of Theology and Philosophy* (January 1984): 6.

21. Meland, "In Response to Miller," 109.

22. Ibid.

23. Ibid., 108.

24. Meland, *Realities of Faith*, 112.

25. Ibid., 114.

26. Ibid.

27. Bernard Meland, "From Darwin to Whitehead," *The Journal of Religion* 40 (October 1960): 240.

28. Bernard Meland, *Seeds of Redemption* (New York: The Macmillan Co., Inc., 1947) 39.

29. Ibid.

30. Ibid.

31. Meland, "From Darwin to Whitehead," 234.

32. Cf. Meland, *Realities of Faith*, 118–119.

33. Ibid., 119–120.

34. Ibid., 120.

35. Bernard Meland, *The Reawakening of Christian Faith* (New York: The Macmillan Co.,, 1949) 51. He quotes from Alfred North Whitehead, *Adventure of Ideas* (New York: The Macmillan Co., 1933) 299.

36. Meland, *Higher Education and Human Spirit*, 40–46.

37. Bernard Meland, "Grace: A Dimension within Nature?" *The Journal of Religion* 54 (1974): 125.

38. Meland, *Higher Education and Human Spirit*, 45.

39. Ibid.

40. Bernard Meland, *Faith and Culture* (New York: Oxford University Press, 1953) 44.

41. Cf. Meland, *Seeds of Redemption*, 155–156.

42. Meland, "Genius of Protestant Thought," 290.

43. Ibid.

44. Cf. Bernard Meland, *Fallible Forms and Symbols* (Philadelphia: Fortress Press, 1976) 134–135.

45. Meland, *Realities of Faith*, 120.

46. Ibid.

47. Ibid.

48. Ty Inbody, "Bernard Meland, A Rebel Among Process Theologians," *American Journal of Theology and Philosophy* 5 (April 1953): 44.

49. Bernard Meland, "Interpreting the Christian Faith within a Philosophical Framework," *The Journal of Religion* 33 (April 1953): 87.

50. Ibid., 89.

51. Ibid., 90.

52. Ibid.

53. Ibid., 91.

54. Ibid., 92.

55. Ibid.

56. Ibid.

57. Ibid.

58. Ibid.

59. Ibid.

60. Ibid.

61. Ibid.

62. Ibid., 94.

63. Meland, *Higher Education and the Human Spirit*, 97.

64. Cf. Meland, *Seeds of Redemption*, 155–156, and Meland, "Interpreting the Christian Faith," 90.

65. Meland, *Seeds of Redemption*, 155.

66. Cf. Meland, *Faith and Culture*, 182. and Bernard Meland, "Toward a Common Christian Faith," *Christendom* 1 (1937): 389–390.

67. Cf. Wieman and Meland, *American Philosophies of Religion*, 89–90; and Meland, *Faith and Culture*, 182.

68. Wieman and Meland, *American Philosophies of Religion*, 85, 87.

69. Meland, *Faith and Culture*, 140.

70. Meland, "The Mystic Returns," The *Journal of Religion* 17 (1937): 155.

71. Ibid.

72. Ibid., 155–156.

73. Bernard Meland, "Some Unresolved Issues in Theology," *The Journal of Religion* 24 (1944): 234.

74. Meland, *Faith and Culture*, 36.

75. Wieman and Meland, *American Philosophies of Religion*, 84.

76. Meland, "Toward a Common Christian Faith," 389.

77. Cf. Bernard Meland, "The Present Issue in Christianity," *The Christian Century* 56 (February 1, 1939): 156-157.

78. Meland, *Faith and Culture*, 182; and Meland, "Present issue in Christianity," 156.

79. Cf. Meland, "Toward a Common Christian Faith," 389.

80. Meland, *Faith and Culture*, 182.

81. Ibid., 183.

82. Ibid.

83. Ibid.

84. Cf. Bernard Meland, "Theology and the Historian of Religion," *The Journal of Religion* 41 (1961): 270.

85. Cf. Meland, *Faith and Culture*, 83–84.

86. Ibid., 84.

87. Ibid.

88. Meland, *Fallible Forms and Symbols*, 105.

89. Ibid.

90. Bernard Meland, "Why Religion?" *The Methodist Quarterly Review* 79 (1930): 360.

91. Meland, *Reawakening of Christian Faith*, 120.

92. Ibid.

93. Ibid., 121.

94. Ibid., 117–118.

95. Ibid., 19.

96. Ibid. 20.

97. Ibid., 21.

98. Ibid.

99. Meland, "Empirical Tradition in Theology," 35.

100. Cf. Meland, *Fallible Forms and Symbols,* 138–139.

101. Cf. Meland, "Empirical Tradition in Theology," 34.

102. Meland, *Higher Education and Human Spirit,* 162.

103. Cf. Meland, *Reawakening of Christian Faith,* 45–47.

104. Cf. *Realities of Faith,* 4–5.

105. Ibid., 105.

106. Cf. Meland, *Fallible Forms and Symbols,* 140.

107. Ibid.

108. Ibid., 141.

109. Ibid.

110. Inbody, "Bernard Meland, Rebel Among Process Theologians," 57.

111. Cf. Meland, *Fallible Forms and Symbols,* 134.

112. Ibid., 135.

113. Ibid.

114. Cf. Ibid.

115. Cf. Meland, *Higher Education and Human Spirit,* 28.

116. Cf. Meland, *Fallible Forms and Symbols,* 135.

117. Meland, "Grace: A Dimension within Nature?" 123.

118. Cf. Meland, *Fallible Forms and Symbols,* 111–112.

119. Ibid.

120. Bernard Meland, "Is God Many or One?" *Christian Century* 100 (1933): 726.

121. Bernard Meland, "Toward a Valid View of God," *Harvard Theological Review* (1931): 203.

122. Ibid., 208.

123. Ibid., 202.

124. Meland, "Appreciative Approach in Religion," 203.

125. Ibid., 204.

126. Cf. Bernard Meland, "Education for a Spiritual Culture," *The Journal of Religion* 26 (1946): 95-96.

127. Meland, *Reawakening of Christian Faith*, viii.

128. Ibid., 6.

129. Meland, *Seeds of Redemption*, 5–7.

130. Ibid., 7.

131. Ibid. And cf. Bernard Meland, *The Secularization of Modern Culture* (New York: Oxford University Press, 1966) 60-66, 68-70, and 72-73 for a more recent exposition of this same theme in regards to Eastern as well as Western cultures.

132. Meland, *Reawakening of Christian Faith*, 34.

133. Meland, *Fallible Forms and Symbols*, 42–43.

134. Cf. Meland, *Reawakening of Christian Faith*, 60–61.

135. Meland, *Seeds of Redemption*, 12.

136. Cf. Bernard Meland, "Seeing God in Human Life," *The Christian Century* 53 (1936): 490.

137. Meland, "The Genius of Protestantism," 281–282.

138. Meland, *Seeds of Redemption*, 25.

139. Ibid.

140. Ibid., 156.

141. Meland, *Higher Education and Human Spirit*, 12.

142. Ibid., 13.

143. Ibid., 25.

144. Ibid., 24.

145. Ibid., 37.

146. Ibid.

147. Ibid., 40.

148. Ibid., 45.

149. Ibid.

150. Ibid.

151. William James, *A Pluralistic Universe* (New York: Longmans, 1911) 307–308. Quoted in Meland, *Faith and Culture*, 48–49.

152. Meland, *Higher Education and Human Spirit*, 45.

153. Ibid., 52.

154. Ibid., 63.

155. Ibid., 64.

156. Ibid.

157. Ibid.

158. Ibid.

159. Meland, *Seeds of Redemption*, 12.

160. Ibid.

161. Gerald J. Janzen, "Meland as Yahwistic Theologian of Culture," *The Journal of Religion* 60 (October 1980): 391.

162. Meland, *Fallible Forms and Symbols*, 28.

163. Meland, *Faith and Culture*, 13.

164. Ibid.

165. Ibid., 15. Discussion 14–15.

166. Ibid., 18.

167. Ibid., 16.

168. Ibid.

169. Meland, *Realities of Faith*, 215.

170. Ibid., 218.

171. Meland, *Faith and Culture*, 69–71.

172. Meland, *Realities of Faith*, 220.

173. Ibid., 221.

174.174. Meland, *Faith and Culture*, 44.

175. Bernard Meland, "Analogy and Myth in Post Liberal Theology," *Process Philosophy and Christian Thought. Eds. Delwin Brown, Ralph E. James, Jr., and Gene Reeves.* (New York: Bobs-Merrill, Co., Inc., 1971), 125.

176. Meland, *Reawakening of Christian Faith*, 65–66.

177. Ibid., 67.

178. Meland, *Faith and Culture*, 55.

179. Meland, "Analogy and Myth," 124.

180. Ibid., 123–124.

181. Ibid., 124.

182. Ibid., 126.

183. Ibid., 127.

184. Ibid.

185. Rudolf Bultmann, *Kerygma and Myth* (New York: Harper Torchbooks, 1961), 24.

186. Ibid., 25.

187. Meland, "Analogy and Myth," 126.

188. Meland, *Faith and Culture*, 28.

189. Meland, *Fallible Forms and Symbols*, 102.

190. Meland, *Reawakening of Christian Faith*, 81,

191. Ibid., 80.

192. Ibid.

193. Ibid.

194. Meland, "From Darwin to Whitehead," 242.

195. Bernard Meland, "New Dimensions of Liberal Faith," *The Christian Century* 74 (1957): 962. Also, cf. Bernard Meland, "Religion has not Lost its Hold," *Religious Education* 21 (July 1935): 29.

196. Meland, *Faith and Culture*, 83–84.

197. Ibid.

198. Meland, *Fallible Forms and Symbols*, 105.

199. Cf. Bernard Meland, "How is Culture a Source for Theology," *Criterion* 3 (1964): 10–21.

200. Meland, *Fallible Forms and Symbols*, 105.

201. Meland, *Faith and Culture*, 178.

202. Ibid.

203. Ibid., 99.

204. Ibid., 96.

205. Ibid.

206. Ibid., 97.

207. Ibid., 109.

208. Ibid.

209. Ibid., 110.

210. Meland, *Seeds of Redemption*, 13.

211. Ibid.

212. Meland, *Faith and Culture.* 37–38.

213. Ibid., 31.

214. Ibid., 35.

215. Meland, *Fallible Forms and Symbols*, 106.

216. Meland, *Faith and Culture*, 37.

217. Meland, *Fallible Forms*, 102–103.

218. Ibid., 116.

219. Ibid., 90. Cf. Ibid., 88–90.

220. Ibid. 90.

221. Ibid., 86.

222. Ibid.

223. Ibid.

224. Ibid., 157.

225. Cf. Ibid., 148–149.

226. Ibid., 95, and Alfred North Whitehead, *Adventures of Ideas* (New York: The Macmillan Co., 1933) 214.

227. Meland, *Fallible Forms and Symbols*, 94.

228. Cf. Meland, "New Dimensions of Liberal Faith," 962.

229. Meland, *Fallible Forms and Symbols*, 96.

230. Cf. Ibid., 94–96, and Meland, *Realities of Faith*, 46–47.

231. Meland, *Fallible Forms and Symbols*, 97.

232. Ibid., 98.

233. Ibid., 98–99.

234. Ibid., 99.

235. Ibid.

236. Ibid., 100.

237. Ibid., 101.

238. Ibid.

239. Ibid.

240. Meland, *Faith and Culture*, 195.

241. Bernard Meland, "In Response to Loomer," *American Journal of Theology and Philosophy* 2 and 3 (May and September 1984): 152.

242. Ibid., 153.

CHAPTER IV

KAPLAN AND MELAND: THEOLOGICAL STRUCTURE

It has already been shown how Kaplan fits into the functional stream within the American Empirical Movement. Using ideas found in the philosophy of John Dewey, Kaplan looks for processes in the universe that correspond to human needs for spiritual fulfillment. Kaplan seeks to isolate those processes or functions that aid in humanity's salvation conceptually so that human effort can be channeled to aid in humanity's salvation.[1]

Meland, on the other hand, fits into the mystical stream. Meland begins with a sense of mystery and depth garnered from the works of William James and uses Whiteheadian concepts to convey clarity of meaning. Meland wants to keep in touch with the rich depth of experience and at the same time find conceptual clarity within possible limits.

Both theologians are concerned with the relation of culture and religion. For them, religion is always inextricably bound to culture. Kaplan thinks of culture in terms of a certain ethnic group, a folk bound by the past and having shared values. In every ethnic group there is a religious dimension. Thus every ethnic group is a religious civilization. For Kaplan, individuals within a culture have basic spiritual needs, needs that are just as basic as the need for food or the need for economic security. These spiritual needs, such as the need to belong, to feel part of an identifiable group "that orients him to existence as a whole,"[2] can only be met within a given cultural community.

For Kaplan, religion grows out of the values and ideals of a given ethnic community or group. Meland thinks of culture as the broader influences of Western history within which an individual asserts personal uniqueness.[3] Meland also notes the interrelation of religion and culture and speaks of the "subtleties of faith as they are woven into a cultural fabric."[4] He applauds human sensitivity and striving for meaning that elicited "the myth making consciousness out of which the early structures of religious experience have emerged."[5]

Both theologians are convinced that religion is rooted in the natural realm and reject the notion that there is a supernatural realm. For both the natural world is so constructed that there are forces written into the natural structure of the cosmos that aid people in their search for self-fulfillment. These forces correspond or are *en rapport* with the basic spiritual needs of humanity. Each culture develops symbols, rituals and a way of life in relation to that in the cosmic structure that aids people in their attempt to find self-fulfillment in community. Kaplan and Meland are in agreement that the structure or process that aids human beings in their attempt to achieve self-fulfillment is more than the mere projection of human values and ideals.

They thus differ from both Dewey and Durkheim in asserting that the "power" at work in the cosmos is objective as well as subjective. There is built into the natural structure of the world a "power" or "powers" that makes for salvation.

They differ, however, in their assessment of the divine nature. Both speak of God as process but Kaplan prefers to portray the forces in the universe that promote human good in terms of impersonal power or process. Meland, in his mature works, speaks of the divine process as the centered other or as person. At a minimum this means that God's interaction with creation, and specifically with humanity, is at the level of consciousness as well as at the level of feeling. Meland cautions against understanding "person" as simply the sum total of human consciousness. God relates to human beings as one person to another but God is not simply human consciousness, and though God relates to individuals, God's essential nature is always a mystery. Meland speaks of the parent-child imagery often used in Christianity as illustrative of the personal relationship that exists between persons and God.

> I believe God to be a reality of grace and judgement which both interpenetrates and transcends the life of man in the way that the hopes and judgments of a father transcend and intermesh with the life of his son. The imagery of parental care which the Hebraic-Christian faith has employed to convey the personal relationship between God and His creatures is sound so long as the imagery is not used to reduce God to human stature and thus to mythologize a meaning which really transcends man's mind even as it cradles and nurtures the whole of man's existence.[6]

Meland and Kaplan differ in their theological method, *i.e.*, in the way in which they go about "studying" God. Kaplan uses a model drawn from the laboratory sciences and applied to social structure. In a laboratory situation one abstracts from the total relational context those aspects that will make a particular experiment work or prove a particular point. Thus in determining what the idea of God should be, Kaplan asks what is necessary in the God-idea if the God-idea is to work to promote human fulfillment. The focus is: how does this structure work within a social setting? What forces or processes work to create value within a given community? Just as one can isolate certain functions that work within a laboratory experiment, so one can isolate those processes or structures within the human and natural environment that people need to create a healthier human community. These processes Kaplan labels God. "When Jewish history and religion are transposed into the key of humanism, God is conceived as the functioning in nature of the eternally creative process."[7]

Meland's method is quite different, drawing its model from images displayed in modern physics, process philosophy and from poetry. From the new physics he learned "that the most intimate penetration of atomic structure revealed electrons existing in a relation of mutuality, behaving, not as independent particles, but as selves in a system."[8] In the works of Alfred North Whitehead and other organismic philosophers he saw an attempt to account for what was revealed by modern physics. "These philosophies undertake the ambitious task of creating in contemporary terms a metaphysical synthesis of the operational realities that will account for the order and integrative activity observed there,"[9] *i.e.*, in modern physics. Poetry was important because in it Meland saw the integration of emotion and reason, without which human self-fulfillment is not possible.[10] Meland attempts to probe the deeper order that surrounds and helps create human existence. He begins not with abstract structure but with perception, a kind of perception that tries to probe not just the external structure but the internal meanings of things and the pervasive depth of meanings that cradles each perceived structure.

Perception is primary because the data is lived experience and not abstractions from experience. In perception, one is dealing both with structure and with the incalculable dimension, with rationality and mystery. The mode of perception that is attentive to the total feeling context is what Meland calls the "appreciative consciousness." At its deepest level the appreciative consciousness becomes faith. For Meland, "faith is thus the capacity in man to sense his human limits by a reason of a sensitivity to what stands over against the human structure of consciousness and over against the human situation."[11]

Kaplan's notion of the way God works in the world and of the relation between humanity and God is clearer and simpler than Meland's. Following Dewey, Kaplan begins with basic human needs and then asks what structure or process in the cosmos makes it possible for a given society to furnish its members with the means for self-fulfillment or salvation. God is correlative to human needs. God is the sum of all values that enhance human life. Though, as we noted above, there is some confusion in his thought over whether God is a unity or an abstract term covering a multiplicity of entities, the fact remains that the term God is applicable to that in society and in the universe that can promote human good. God is the tool that humanity can use to further human good. The obvious assumption that runs through Kaplan's thought is that the universe and people are so constructed that that which is good for human self-fulfillment is in accord with cosmic good. "Divinity is that aspect of the whole of nature, both in the universe and in man, which impels humanity to create a better and happier world and every individual to make the most of his own life."[12] The universe at its best is basically friendly to humanity. Persons need only to assess what is morally best for society and can with confidence then proceed to implement changes needed because they know that what they are doing is basically in harmony with the highest elements of the universe.

Meland is inclined to subsume the ethical category under the aesthetic and to see discontinuities as well as continuities between human needs and God's workings. His doctrine of God's working in the world or of the immanence of God "simply presupposes that there are structures within the reach and recognition of man which disclose God's working in some form and to some degree."[13] His thought centers not on human needs and values but on the imaginative grasp of the ultimate that a society expresses in its "mythos." For Meland, "each culture exemplifies the concrete nature of God's working within the range of its available structures."[14] The mythos contains seminal notions or root metaphors that express the feeling context and intellectual thrust of a given culture. These primal notions arise from the work of both

God and humanity. They are the results of the interaction between God and human beings within a given cultural context and they act as a formative agent to future cultural expression.

Whereas Kaplan sees a clear correspondence between human needs and God's work, Meland is much more tentative in his conclusion. He speaks of trust and hope based on the resources of grace that come to us within a given culture rather than on an intellectual grasp of definite function.

> At best, through the most disciplined and persistent efforts, with adequate sensibility as to what is beyond comprehension, conceivably beyond our apprehension, we may aspire to a degree of intelligibility and encouragement to persist in the act of faith in a mood of trust and openness to such intimations of insight beyond the assured sense of intelligibility as these lived experiences may yield."[15]

Kaplan is concerned with translating the basic insights of his tradition into a modern idiom. Kaplan does this through what he calls revaluation. "Revaluation consists in disengaging from the traditional context those elements in it which answer permanent postulates of human nature and in integrating them into our own ideology."[16] These revalued or reinterpreted notions then serve the modern person seeking to both draw from the past and create ideals for the future.

Meland, while attentive to the intellectual currents of our age, argues that there are some fundamental mythic insights that cannot be translated into a current scientific, psychological or philosophical idiom. God as person, and the saving act of God in history are two such fundamental mythical statements that cannot be translated. For Meland, these two notions are so fundamental to the shaping of Western culture that even those who deny them are unable to shake the lingering vestiges of them in their thought.[17] The preservation and strengthening of the religious-ethnic community of which he is a member is explicitly of major importance for Kaplan. Therefore, he is very concerned with community organization and structure, proposing many programs that should aid in the revitalizing of the community. Aside from some early attention to the problem of worship, Meland's work is much less practically oriented. His concern for showing how the Christian mythos has shaped Western culture has led him to neglect institutional structure and community organization. It is not that he does not think that these concerns are important, but the thrust of his thought has focused on the impact of the Christian witness beyond the borders of the particular community of which he is a member.

In all the formal agreements and differences listed above, we have not as yet looked at those aspects of their thought which are related to each theologians specific religious tradition. In the next section we will focus on three fundamental questions and show how the answers to these questions are shaped, for each of our writers, by the tradition from which he comes. The questions are: "How is salvation mediated?" "What is the relation between God and humanity?" and "How is God imaged?"

Influence of the Traditions

1.   How is Salvation Mediated?

The basic Jewish orientation of Kaplan's thought is revealed in his answer to this question. For him this question can only be answered in terms of the corporate existence of a given community and for him that means the corporate existence of the Jewish people with a given way of life or Torah. Kaplan argues that salvation shorn of its otherworldly accretions means self-fulfillment within a given ethnic community. In *Judaism as a Civilization* he speaks of the role of the Jewish community in salvation in the following manner:

> As a civilization, Judaism is that dynamic pattern of life which enables the Jewish people to be a means of salvation to the individual Jew. In the past when salvation meant attainment of bliss in the hereafter, the Jewish civilization was other-worldly in its entire outlook, content and motivation.[18]

The modern world, however, is totally different in outlook, denying the very possibility of an afterlife, still the Jewish community can nonetheless act as a medium of salvation for its members.

> Now when salvation depends on making the most of the opportunities presented by this world, the form of social organization, the language, literature, religion, laws, folkways and art must so function that through them the Jewish people will help to make the life of the Jew creative and capable of self-fulfillment.[19]

According to Kaplan's understanding, a group religion, such as Judaism, is best understood through values. He uses the term "wisdom" for that category of values which orients the community to the goal of salvation or self-fulfillment. Wisdom, as a category, is not based on reason or on verifiable facts but on the satisfaction of spiritual needs. These spiritual needs, which separate human beings from the lower animals, "are the needs for controlling and directing human efforts in satisfying biological needs without indulgence in lust and in satisfying psycho-social needs without surrender to greed."[20] The need for control and direction means that "the individual requires involvement with his self-governing, self-perpetuating organic community, such as a family, clan, tribe, nation or people."[21] Kaplan sums up his position in the following words.

Hence, man's spiritual needs can be met only among those who pursue a common way of life, speak the same language and communicate in the same universe of thought and discourse. The common good of the organic community requires that the individual drives of its constituents must not should not overpower the well-being of others. In his striving for competence or power the individual must be restrained from greed and aggression.[22]

When a community legislates the way in which its members should live in accordance with the above requirements, the members develop a group consciousness or mind and will.

In order for Judaism to offer salvation for its members in accordance with present day needs, it is necessary that changes be made "in its ideology, sanctions, practices and social organization."[23] These should not be random changes of everything that seems out of step with the modern world. All changes are subject to three basic criteria. The changes must not destroy the community's sense of continuity with the past. This means study of the history of the people and the Torah as well as an attitude of honor for the land from which the people emerged as a national group. The changes must not undermine its unique individuality. The changes must not be in the direction of so intermingling with the larger nations or societies that the Jewish community's own distinctiveness is lost; communication, yes, but not assimilation to the point that Jewish identity is forsaken. Further, the changes must not destroy its organic character. That is, the relationship between people, law, and the divine must be maintained. Religion cannot be divorced from the life and culture of the people.

When Judaism as a civilization is reconstituted so that it conforms with the modern world view and yet maintains the values of the ethnic community, then it will function as a means of salvation for each individual Jew, for each individual "has to be part of a fellowship that orients him to existence as a whole, otherwise he feels rootless."[24] Kaplan notes that this need to belong to a fellowship that provides inspiration and guidance for its members has a spiritual character. Indeed, spirituality means feeling at home in a community that gives meaning to existence. It is only in such a community or fellowship that "a person learns to be and do the best of which he is capable, and to bear without bitterness the worst that can befall him."[25]

Kaplan is not unaware that the modern Jew has the option of joining other national and ecclesiastical communions that could offer similar opportunities for self-fulfillment as does the Jewish community. National communism, for example, offers salvation or self-fulfillment and demands total commitment to its way of life. Only by cutting himself off from the ethnic and religious past can a Jew become a first-class citizen in a communist country. Kaplan points out, however, that in the United States, as in other Western societies where the state does not claim to have the capacity for providing salvation for its members, the only viable alternative for the individual Jew is to become a Christian. This course is not possible for the average Jew according to Kaplan because it "would be doing violence to his intellectual integrity."[26]

One example, which Kaplan gives to show how the Jews' intellectual integrity would be violated, is what Kaplan understands as the Christian notion of depravity. Kaplan sees this notion as basic to Christian thought. Jews would do violence to their integrity by accepting the notion of inherent depravity in humanity. The Jew, though aware of how much easier it often seems to be to do the wrong rather than the right, knows that individuals can choose to do good without any help from supernatural grace or a Christ.[27] Perhaps, more importantly, from the standpoint of Kaplan's basic concern, becoming a Christian would cut the Jew off from all the rich traditions of the past that have given a unique character to the way in which the individual

Jew perceives life. Joining a Christian community, like joining a Communist community, would cut the individual Jew off from the values and ideals that to a great extent have formed the Jew's personality. Furthermore, the Jew would be joining a community that has denounced the people and way of life that have nurtured this unique individuality and aided it on the way to maturity. Finally, of course, Kaplan thinks that even in a liberal country like America, the forces of anti-semitism are so strong that Jews would not be permitted to join the Christian community *en masse*. For the Jew, the only practical and viable vehicle for salvation is one's own People. The Jewish ethnic-religious community is the only place where the modern Jew can retain meaningful links with the past and find a meaningful way of life in the present. As Kaplan says, "The religious rationale for Judaism must, therefore, be the desire to make of our Jewish heritage that which can elicit the best that is in us."[28]

Salvation for the Jew, as Kaplan sees it, is always conditioned upon the existence of the Jewish community.

> No individual is spiritually self-sufficient. The meaning and values that life has for him are a result of his relationship to the civilization in which he participates. The more that civilization functions as a way of salvation, the more intense will be the individual's sense of identification with it, and the realization of its worth, or its "holiness."[29]

Kaplan's understanding of salvation may differ from others within the Jewish tradition, from those in the past who held that otherworldly salvation could only be obtained if one belonged to the Jewish community, but he, like them, maintains that the community is indispensable for salvation. Personal salvation, according to Kaplan, "represents the faith in the possibility of achieving an integrated personality."[30] This personal salvation cannot be achieved without reference to a social objective. "Selfish salvation is an impossibility, because no human being is psychologically self-sufficient."[31] Salvation for the individual is dependent on "the ultimate achievement of a social order in which all men shall collaborate in the pursuit of common ends in a manner which shall afford to each the maximum opportunity for creative self-expression."[32] Since he and the older tradition are both convinced of the salvitic significance of the ethnic community, Kaplan sees himself as solidly bound to the Jewish tradition, even though the older tradition assumed that the community was necessary to assure a supernatural salvation and Kaplan assumes that the community is necessary for individual self-fulfillment.

For Meland, redemption or salvation is the sensitive appreciation of the resources of grace and goodness unleashed in the world in the Christ. Both the church (the cultus) and the culture within the Western ethos point "to the living Christ as a continuing work of the New Creation, revealing the Infinite Structure of grace and judgment in each generation of history."[33] The church and the wider cultural community are both important as mediators of grace and goodness to the individual, but they are important because they point to and are witnesses to the primary mediator of God's grace for Western people, the Christ. This Christ is not for Meland simply a remembered event. It is a fact of immediate experience.

> Our faith, we may be startled to find, is not just a faith in the scriptural memory of the Christ-event, not just a symbolic transfer from an ancient to a modern idiom, but faith in the reality of a New Creation that meets us in every event of betrayal or blessedness, in every experience of sin and forgiveness, in every encounter with defeat and despair, and in the joys of the resurrected life that follows again and again upon this experience of judgment and grace as we mingle with our fellows, of whatever confession, or of no confession, and as we stumble into or out of the stark, tragedy-laden events of these harrowing experiences of present-day history.[34]

It is this revelation of God in Christ that released into human culture a redemptive power that

> continues to release men from their restrictive egoism as well as from the mechanisms of their own humanly contrived orders of logic and justice, enabling them to participate, in part, in this more sensitive order of meaning, despite the dominating frustration of their characteristically human structures.[35]

The church at its best is the focal point in the culture of witness to this Christ event. Often, however, as Meland sees it, the church has itself been an offence to the Christian faith. It becomes an offense when it substitutes political power for the gentle power of goodness displayed in Christ.

Salvation for Meland then is not primarily well-being within a community but an immediate experience of grace released by the Christ-event. Those who acknowledge their commitment to the Christ form a witnessing community, the church, but the Christ is not contained within the cultus and not all who experience the Christ do so within the confines of the cultus. The church community and the larger cultural community are important in the life of the believer, but finally salvation is determined by an individual's sensitivity to the Christ and to grace and goodness released by the Christ-event, and not by attainment of self-fulfillment within a community.

In spite of the basic difference in emphasis of their thought, they are in agreement on the positive evaluation of culture. For both culture, either as an ethnic community (Kaplan) or through its mythos (Meland), is the medium of salvation. Neither Kaplan nor Meland would accept the notion that salvation comes from outside of or beyond culture. Both stress the immanence of God at work in the world and in culture and in the experience of the individual. Where they differ Kaplan sees the individual as relating to God through the ethnic community whereas Meland sees the Christ event as determinative of salvation for each individual. Redemption, becoming more sensitive to the resources of grace unleashed in the Christ event, may lead an individual to identify more closely with the cultic community witnessing to the Christ-event. However, both Western culture and the cultic community are shaped by the Christian mythos' emphasis on the relation of the individual to God. This emphasis on the Christ as the mediator of salvation versus the emphasis on the corporate ethnic community as the mediator of salvation, marks the distinctively Christian versus the distinctly Jewish understanding.

2.   What is the Relationship between God and Humanity?

For both Kaplan and Meland, the metaphor for relationship between God and humanity is covenant. Kaplan emphasizes that even in his modern re-interpre-tation the "covenant" is to be understood as between God and the entire Jewish people or nation. "Ancient Israel's covenant relation to God should be understood in humanist terms as committing the entire Jewish people to ethical nationhood."[36] Although in his later writings,[37] Kaplan held that one could not reinterpret or revaluate the notion of chosenness at all because of the long-standing literalistic interpretations of that doctrine by both Judaism and Christianity, in his earlier *Judaism as a Civilization*, he revalued the ideas of election and covenant. The essential meanings that come out of his revalua-tion are not repudiated in his later writings even when he found it necessary to give up the use of the word election or chosenness. For traditional Jews, according to Kaplan, the covenant between God and Israel was seen as the result of special divine election. At Mt. Sinai the Jews were offered the covenant and they accepted it. Further, as Kaplan sees it, it was because of this belief that they were chosen by God and had entered into an agreement with God, that the Jews endured as a cohesive group throughout the ages in spite of persecution and the loss of their homeland. As he says,

> of the conscious factors which formerly contributed to the survival of the Jews in the face of systematic persecution and oppression, first place is undoubtedly to be assigned to the belief that they were the special object of divine providence, a belief held alike by the sophisticated and the naive.[38]

It is no longer possible for the Jewish people to understand their nationhood as a result of such special attention by the divine. He emphasizes that the Jewish people must accept the fact that other nations live by divine ideals. Thus any attempt at reconstruction must reject any notion of national superiority. On the other hand, the rejection of the notion of national superiority does not mean that it is not possible to construct new meanings that will justify the retention of the Jews as a particular national entity and stay true to the permanent human truths embodied in the notions of election and covenant. The notion of election gave to the traditional Jewish people their purpose and value. Today, according to Kaplan, "Jews must find within the scope and functioning of their very nationhood something that would endow it in their own eyes with purpose and value."[39]

This can only be done through the method of functional revaluation of the notions of election and covenant. Functional revaluation takes place when "we analyze or break up the traditional values into their implications, and single out for acceptance those implications which can help us meet our own moral and spiritual needs."[40] Kaplan begins with an historical analysis of the time and situation out of which these doctrines emerged. The ancient Jews were limited by their historical situation and their oriental cast of mind when they tried to put into language their basic experiences. Thus they used the notion of election to express the fact that there was something essentially meaningful and important about their nation. Like other ancient peoples, their thought took the form of deeply held convictions arising out of the circumstances of their existence. These convictions were not based on abstract principles or abstract modes of thought and thus could not be readily transferred to other nations or peoples.[41]

He suggests that the notion of election arose in the following way. The Jews, intuitively, within the historical context of which they were a part, sensed the power for good that adhered in the moral ideal. Since they could not imagine themselves as having conceived of and chosen to live by the highest moral ideals, they imagined an allegiance to a deity who had chosen them. "Shelled out of the mode of thought and expression natural to the oriental mind, the kernel ideal of the doctrine of divine election of Israel is that nationhood brings into play forces and events in the life of a group which enable its member to achieve self-fulfillment."[42] Election as a revalued concept means that the Jews chose to form a nationhood that uniquely allowed human beings to achieve their highest good. This revalued concept is the one that can and should be meaningful within the modern world.

In traditional Judaism the covenant (as expressed in Torah which embodied the terms of election) was understood as given by God and agreed upon by the people. The covenant was seen as having come down directly from God. This constitution or code of laws holding this particular people together was not understood in the way in which Kaplan understands it, as arising out of a nation's struggle to maintain justice and to create a society that would enhance and further human potential. Rabbinic Judaism saw this Torah or code of laws as constituting "the principle instrument which confers nationhood upon the Jews."[43] The nationhood of the Jews was conditioned by the manner of life and the mode of living that was set forth in the Torah. Kaplan affirms that it is the ideals embodied in the Torah that gave Jewish civilization its moral and spiritual character, but he sees these ideals as having arisen out of the need of a people to live in harmony with each other. He does not accept the rabbinic notion that the laws governing national conduct were given *en toto* at Mt. Sinai.[44]

Revaluation consists in accepting the Torah as foundational for the continuation of Jewish civilization from three perspectives: from the perspective of symbol, from the perspective of its content, and from the perspective of a process. "As a covenant, The Torah is a symbol, representing the truth that a nation becomes such not through the accident of common ancestry or physical propinquity, but through the consent of those who constitute it to live together and to make their common past the inspiration for a common future."[45] The covenant stands as a symbol of the spiritual bond uniting a people, and the expression of the general will of the collective personality of a people.

The Torah is the symbol of a nation's unified consensus about spiritual and ethical values. Understood in terms of content, the Torah contains all the basic principles necessary for a national civilization. The basic principles of this national civilization are not based on power but on cultural and moral purposes. Sovereign power, power based on armies and on force, would be replaced in ethical nationhood by humanitarian purpose. The Torah lays down rules for ethical and religious conduct; it lays down the foundation for a judicial system and it even deals with matters of common courtesy or etiquette. The blueprint for civilization or nationhood contained within the Torah is not based on power over others and the putting down of the weak, but its basis is the "urge to develop those human differentiae and potentialities which only collective life can bring forth."[46] Torah, understood as process, emphasizes the importance of education. In Kaplan's understanding, education is just as important when Torah is understood as a process as it was when Torah was understood as a finished plan. This is so because the basic principles of morality and values embodied in the Torah need to be understood and applied in light of today's circumstances. Education not only tells one what the Torah meant for the past, it should provide the basic principles for existence in the present and future. Thus revaluation does not mean that education can be neglected. The Torah, as a living process, contains those principles of morality and values that are passed on through the tradition from teacher to pupil, from parent to child. Nothing within a community should be allowed to stand in the way of this important function—of passing significant knowledge from one generation to another. Without education that makes one aware of ones roots in the past, and the values that shape one's community, it is impossible for an individual human being to realize his or her full potential, and it is impossible for a community to provide further laws that will be applicable to the present without cutting itself off from its past.[47]

Torah or covenant is not the statement of otherworldly or abstract principles but a practical, spiritual and moral document meant to guide a community. By accepting the Torah as a moral covenant the Jews are committed to seeing it implemented within the life of the community.

> The Jews are bound to develop social agencies which will demonstrate to the world that the main function of states and governments is not to exercise police power in defense of the economic and political *status quo*, but to create such laws and institutions as would enable those who are identified with the nation to bring to fruition whatever powers for the good they possess.[48]

On the basis of the concrete ideals embodied in the Torah it will be possible for economic and political institutions to evolve so that they will create justice and righteousness in society.

Election and covenant in their revalued form mean "that the dedication of a people to God's purposes is the highest vocation to which any group can aspire," to use the words of Jack J. Cohen in "Kaplan's Concept of People-hood."[49] Through the process of revaluation, election and partaking of the covenant become the vocation by which a people dedicates itself to furthering human good within a society. This idea of covenant differs markedly from the traditional understanding. As was noted above, the idea of election and entering into the covenant originally implied for the Jewish people, the entering into a special pact with a transcendent, supernatural God. In Kaplan's revaluation, the supernatural God is removed, and the Jewish nation becomes a people who dedicate themselves to the highest ideals of human-social development. On a practical level, entering the covenental pact becomes the decision of the Jewish people to work towards a better future based on universal principles that will satisfy basic human needs and enhance human values.[50] Since, as Kaplan acknowledges, there is a real difference between his understanding of the covenant relation and the understanding which has been normative for the tradition, it is important to make clear his divergence from the tradition. Originally, the idea of election and entering into a covenant implied that the Jewish people entered into a special pact with a supernatural, transcendent God. In Kaplan's revaluation, however, "when Jewish history and religion are transported into the key of humanism, God is conceived as the functioning in nature of the eternally creative process, which, by bringing order out of chaos and good out of evil, actuates man to self-fulfillment."[51] Thus, in Kaplan's revaluation, the supernatural God is removed. The people dedicate themselves to those transnatural values inherent in the cosmos that aid humanity in achieving self-fulfillment. The Jewish nation in Kaplan's schema become a people who dedicate themselves to the highest ideals of human-social development. Entering the covenental pact becomes the decision of the Jewish people to work towards a better future based on universal principles that will satisfy basic human needs and enhance human values.

Ancient Israel's covenant relation to God should be understood in humanist terms as committing the entire Jewish people to ethical nationhood. Just as in the ancient polytheistic world the Israelite nation dedicated itself to the promulgation of ethical monotheism, so in the modern world the Jewish people must undertake the mission of ethical nationhood as a means of international cooperation.[52]

Other nations with ethnic backgrounds other than Jewish can enter into similar covenants. They can do so because the idea of human fulfillment is not necessarily confined to Judaism. Kaplan recommends that each national or ethnic group dedicate itself to the furtherance of spiritual values from their own perspective. As he sees it, his revalued notion of election and covenant is not only applicable to Jews, but he is of course mainly interested in Jewish civilization and it is to and for that organic community that he is primarily speaking.[53]

Kaplan is concerned that his revalued notion of election provide a basis of unity for all Jews, no matter what their socio-economic class or educational standing. He does not assume that the vocation of furthering human values (the revalued notion of election) demands a classless society or a monolithic lifestyle. Among Jews, the covenant would simply demand a common desire among people from widely different theological, philosophical, social and economic situations to dedicate themselves to the creation of a society that would seek to create and implement the highest goals and values for human society.

There must be a place in the Jewish community for every one who wishes to be a Jew, regardless of his theology or economic condition. Jews should not compel uniformity of belief and opinion which would impede progress.[54]

As can be readily seen, Kaplan's revaluation of the notion of covenant is consistent with the notions of social functionalism derived from the thought of John Dewey. For Dewey, ideals are plans or instruments for changing social conditions. The term God refers to those forces and ideals in society that function to change human society for the better. Correspondingly, values are only realized within a social context. Kaplan's revalued covenant reaffirms the importance of the social group and emphasizes the need for the group to aspire to high ideals. The revaluated covenant, like Dewey's thought, stresses the importance of education and the need for human beings to seek their full potential as human beings within the social context. The revalued covenant emphasizes the need for the group to strengthen those ideals that work for the regeneration of human society. Kaplan, in his seeking for a way to make Judaism a viable entity within the modern world, has appropriated from the empirical tradition Dewey's emphasis on social groups. He has also appropriated Dewey's notion that values and ideals, even the ideal of God, grow out of the needs of social groups. By focusing on values and ideals as the product of social groups, Kaplan was enabled to understand and defend the continued existence of the Jewish nation as an ethical-religious community.

Bernard Meland's understanding of the covenant relationship is much more individualistic than Kaplan's. Meland is explicitly conscious of the difference between the understanding of Christian thought and the ancient Hebraic understanding. As we have seen in the above section, Mordecai Kaplan's thought is closer in this regard to the ancient Hebrew understanding than is Meland's. Meland comments on the differences between the Hebraic and the Christian understanding of covenant in the following passage.

> Now it should be noted that, in its more primitive, Hebraic setting, personality was a communal term. The individual acquired and conveyed his distinctive, personal identity and expressiveness through the communal experience and history, and was therefore

representative of the community. Thus, in speaking of God and
man in this context, one was speaking of God and his people.

The individuation of this relationship, making it a metaphorical
commentary upon the nature of man, is of later origin and was to
become dominant in Christian imagery.[55]

Even when discussing the basic Covenant given at Sinai, Meland's
interpretation emphasizes the personal and individual rather than the social-na-
tional elements. The covenental "relationship defines man as being really free
as an individual person, yet responsible to God and to other men."[56] For
Meland, the covenental relationship understood in individualistic terms underlies the prevailing notion in Western experience "that the individual has a
special significance and destiny."[57] The importance and significance of the
individual has been expressed in many different ways throughout the history
of Western thought, "ranging from a concern for the redemption of the
individual to an emphasis upon the primacy of the person in the ethical
sense."[58]

What Meland calls "the root metaphor", *i.e.*, the covenant relationship,
"presents individual men and women as being related to one another through
God in a personal bond of community, thus giving meaning to the individual,
even as it gives dignity and status as a free being."[59] This root metaphor has
metaphysical, legal, and personal implications. Understood in metaphysical
terms, the covenant was translated into the problem of the "One and the
Many." Using a Whiteheadian imagery, the covenant shows the interrelation-
ship between God and humanity or God and the world in the following
manner. God as primordial depends on the multiplicity of the world for the
experience of novelty. When the multiplicity of the world acquires a conceptual unity or oneness it depends upon God for that oneness. God in primordial
nature is unity or one, in consequent nature many. The world, on the other

hand, is primordially many and only in relation to God does it achieve oneness. Religiously, this means that God in the covenant is shown as the primordial one who provides each individual with an ideal of self-realization; and each individual by fulfilling this ideal end adds to the enjoyment and future harmony of God. Whatever else this imagery means, it implies that each individual "embodies God, and is embodied in God."[60] The important point in relation to Meland, is to remember that the emphasis is on individuals who attain community in God. The emphasis is not on a community relation with God in which individuals share.

Meland sees the Western notion of justice as based on the covenental imagery of the primacy of personal relations. From this metaphor, which expresses personal and loving relations, comes the deep sense of justice which permeates Western culture. Unlike the type of justice that arises from Greek thought and which is codified in Roman law—the kind of justice in which the abstract individual is treated exactly like all other individuals—the notion of justice arising out of the Judeo-Christian "covenant" stresses that each person deserves an individual "due." This "due" is not to be understood in terms of simple cause and effect, but is always conditioned upon the specific claims of this particular individual within a context of loving relationships. The claims or rights of the person override any suggestion of inexorable causation. In the New Covenant, which Meland sees as an extension and fuller expression of the Mosaic Covenant, the focus is on the freedom and responsibility of the individual in specific circumstances and not on mechanical observance or simple cause and effect.[61]

The New Covenant means, for Meland, understanding the root covenant metaphor in relation to the Christ event. That event emphasizes the individual person standing in relationship to sin and forgiveness, judgment and love. Love, which is the operative meaning of the New Covenant, "broke upon the

world of Western culture as a result of these elemental Christian happenings
in which the primitive Christian community experienced the impact of these
events centering in the Christ."[62] Those elemental happenings which are both
symbolic and revelatory of the primacy of love are for the Christian, the life,
death and resurrection of the Christ. For Meland, law is not abolished but
transcended by personal relationships that take into account not only infraction
of the law, sin, or the breaking of the covenant, but the willingness of God to
forgive. "The juxtaposition of sin and forgiveness yields a new relationship in
which grace abounds, offering new resources of spirit and a new level of
freedom."[63] This is not a freedom from relationships but a freedom in relationships; the fundamental relationship is that which allows the person to see
oneself as related to God in bonds of love and because of this to be free to
relate to other people in love.[64]

The root metaphor of covenant underlies the Christian understanding of
"the *Imago Dei* (the image of God in the individual)."[65] The covenental
relationship underlying the imagery maintains a distinction between God and
the individual.

> Man is really human. And the distinction between humanity and
> divinity is judiciously observed. This relationship is personal,
> implying freedom, decision, and responsibility in human acts.[66]

In *Faith and Culture* Meland, drawing on Whitehead, focuses on the meaning
for the individual of the *imago dei*. In his discussion of what it means for a
human being to be born or enter into concrete existence, he speaks of three
ways in which the human being is actualized; in relation to God, in relation
to an already existing world, and in relation to his or her own "I." The
human being is never a simple biological existent but always takes on the
character of significance or meaning. The *imago dei* is the creative intent of
God—an expectation which is laid upon each person "by reason of the

creative hand which has shaped this emergent into a concrete event."[67] God impresses on each individual at the level of feeling "an impulse toward love."[68] The sensitivities within each individual that make it possible for that person to live for others as well as for self are the result of the image of God in humanity.

> These sensitivities which awaken the human creature to imagina-
> tive and creative venturing beyond the level of sheer well-being
> or to acts of dedication or of long-suffering, however the course
> of life may run, are qualities of our emergent structure which give
> evidence in our natures of the image of God at the level of
> feeling. In this sense, we are made for God. Whether conscious or
> not of this creative intention which permeates our every moment
> of existence, we bear its imprint upon our natures, if only in the
> form of ambiguous feelings or impulsions which restrain or
> complicate our egoistic will to live unto ourselves.[69]

Kaplan drew on notions found in the works of John Dewey for his revaluation of the covenant. From Dewey he took the notion of the impor-tance of social structure and the group. From Dewey he took the notion that values grew out of needs that people have in accommodating themselves to their environment and society. He also learned from the philosopher to think of ideals as plans for social action and of the unification of the highest ideals as God. Kaplan applied these notions to the "covenant." For him, the cove-nant grew out of the needs and ideals of a given people. The unity of the highest ideals, Kaplan termed God. People could cooperate with God or that which was divine in the universe to aid in their self-fulfillment. The "cove-nant relationship" meant that people could cooperate with those forces in the universe that aided them in producing a better society and a more harmonious way of life for each individual. In his understanding of the "covenant" Meland, on the other hand, is obviously drawing on Whitehead's thought. God, for Whitehead, provides the initial ideal goal for every event and every event prehends both God and the rest of creation in varying degrees of relevance. Through the use of this modern idiom to point to the relation between God and individual persons, Meland is able to focus on persons as individuals in a way that is consistent with his understanding of the Christian tradition. Furthermore, he is able to give voice to his understanding of the radical immanence of God, "the God With us," Immanuel of the New Testament, for in Whiteheadian terms God is radically with every individual creature in each advance into newness.

3.   How is God Imaged?

The last question we will deal with is "How is God imaged?" Mordecai Kaplan has provided a very suggestive insight into how different religious communities envision the idea of God. He says, "Whatever constitutes salvation for the religious community determines the idea of God which the religion of that community professes."[70] Based on this statement then, Kaplan should use images of God which correlate with the notion of group salvation and Meland should use images of God which correlate with a notion of individual salvation. When we turn to Kaplan's images of God we find that he does indeed use images that posit a correlation between God and a people.

> The term "God" belongs to the category of *functional* nouns. Gold, silver, wood, are *substantive* nouns, but teacher, shepherd, king, are *functional* nouns. A functional noun is necessarily correlative: one is a teacher of a pupil, a shepherd of a herd, king or God of a people.[71]

As was noted above, Kaplan rejects the notion of God as a personal being, so when he speaks of God as king he is not suggesting that there is some personal monarch overseeing the world from a transcendent realm. "If

God, conceived as function denotes whatever is of ultimate value to mankind, He cannot be represented as a personal being infinite in power and goodness, which is a contradiction in terms."[72] What is important to Kaplan in the image of King is power, "the Power that evokes personality in men and nation."[73] By responding to the highest ethical or cosmic standards, a nation responds to the power or life of the universe. A nation is not a passive agent in God's hands, and God is not an absolute ruler in the oriental sense, rather God is a monarch who depends on the people. God governs through the people when they choose to live on a high moral plane. "In this sense, God still governs the nation, and the nation still establishes His Kingdom."[74] In *The Meaning of God in Modern Jewish Religion*, Kaplan gives an extensive treatment of the idea of God as king. Kaplan acknowledges that the modern individual would find it difficult to apply this metaphor to God. He justifies the use of this metaphor because of its extensive use within the tradition. What he attempts to do in his discussion of God as King is to find the literal truths that this ancient metaphor conveys. Because of ancient Israel's belief that the God they served was the only one God of the universe and because under the influence of the prophets they came to conceive of this God as "the Source and Sponsor of the moral law,"[75] they accentuated within their society "the primacy of a just social order."[76] This just social order could only be maintained by subscribing to "the highest ethical standards of the nation, as reflected in its interpretation of Torah."[77] God in ancient Israel was seen as the author of Torah, and in the notion of "the Day of Yahweh" there was the further understanding that God would wreck vengeance on those who did not follow divine law and create a new social order. These two notions of God as providing moral law and judgment on the world are revalued by Kaplan to reveal their essential truth, which is that God is the power that makes for social regeneration. In our modern day and age, when sovereignty rarely resides in the Western countries in the hands of an absolute monarch, we still retain a notion of sovereign power. This sovereign power does not operate at the whim of one individual but does operate effectively as "the interaction of personalities of all the individuals of the State in their relation to one another and to the political institutions of their social heritage."[78]

Just as we have changed the meaning of sovereign power in the political realm, so we ought to change our way of viewing the power of God in a religious sense.

> We must identify the sovereignty of God not with the expression of the will of a superhuman, immortal and infallible individual personality, but with that Power on which we rely for the regeneration of society and which operates through individual human beings and social institutions.[79]

Faith is no longer dependent on belief in a God who stands apart from people. "Faith in the sovereignty of God comes then to mean faith that in mankind there is manifest a Power which, in full harmony with the nature of the physical universe, operates for the regeneration of human society."[80] This Power or moral impetus in the universe can only work in society through people. Individuals must dedicate themselves to the improvement of society in order for God's kingship to be actualized. "From the point of view of the sovereignty of God as immanent in human society, the responsibility for ushering in the Kingdom of God on earth rests squarely with mankind."[81] The power of God is manifest in society when human beings actualize the power in their own lives that corresponds with the Cosmic Power. God's sovereignty means making the world liveable, on the physical, social and spiritual level.

Because of his insistence that people must work with God or that in nature which produces ethical nations, Kaplan is against any extreme form of asceticism that assumes that the power of God lies in working against or denying essential human nature. He is equally against any type of theological understanding that would make the actualization of God's sovereign power simply an act of grace on the part of God. For Kaplan, the establishment of God's Kingdom on earth "demands no revolutionary change in human nature itself and no saving act of Providence."[82] Bringing in the kingdom of God or actualizing God's power does demand "specific changes in the factors that condition human life."[83] The demand is for improved physical, social, mental and spiritual conditions. These conditions are improved in the belief or the hope that people's chances of self-fulfillment will be enhanced. Faith is not in people as they actually are but in people as they can become when they utilize the power of God in their lives and in their society. It is the faith, that in spite of the chaos and the seeming sinfulness of life, by aligning themselves with the moral impulse in the universe, people can be redeemed. Accepting the fact that people can improve is for Kaplan, accepting the kingship of God. "The religious outlook on life which is expressed in the conception of the sovereignty of God is an idealistic one affirming the power of men to transform human life in accordance with ideal objectives."[84]

Through the image of God as king, Kaplan has again given expression to his fundamental notion that religion is basically a group phenomenon for, by definition, a king relates not to another individual but to the people as a whole. The notion of God as king or sovereign power also allows Kaplan to focus on those things in society that need to be brought in line with the notion of divine kingship. It gives society objective goals to work for, goals derived from the basic needs of humanity and from the highest aspects of the universe.

If Kaplan's God can be said to be more specifically correlated with social needs, with the forces or power in the universe that creates human good within a societal context,[85] Meland's God is imaged in much more personal and individualistic ways. This distinction, though a valid one, is not an absolute one. Kaplan, of course, speaks of the individual and God, and Meland, of course, speaks of the community and God, but whereas Kaplan emphasizes that the good life for the individual comes through the community and through the community to God, Meland emphasizes the reality of the individual who relates to God and through God to other human beings. This leads Meland to emphasizes not God as ruler but God under the image of a simple human being. God in concreteness is not imaged by Meland as abstract power, not even moral power, but as a single individual who lived in the first century. Meland images God as the Christ, as an individual who enters into the life of other individuals. For Meland, Christology means seeing "God in his concreteness, God reconciling the world unto himself, God taking upon himself the form and burden of actuality, God becoming man, enjoying the simple joys of a carpenters's family or the rugged pleasures in the fisherman's community, alternately partaking of the solitude of the open sea or the arduous climb of some steep ascent."[86] To understand God through the Christ image is to envisage "deity not in its majesty and power as supreme ruler, but as suffering servant, taking up the cross of humanity that is borne by all who suffer from the insensitivities of creaturely existence, both those of their own making and those of others' with whom their life is cast."[87] God is imaged in terms of limitation, in terms of living and dying, in terms of deprivation and loss. "As a result of the vision of existence that has come to us out of the travail of history, the very depiction of Jesus Christ as the Suffering Servant becomes a compelling symbol of the gentle might that transforms and saves in the face of the most formidable threats of our existence."[88] For Meland, the church, or the witnessing community comes into existence in relation to this vision of God at work in Christ. It comes into existence out of "the realiza-

tion that the grace that is offered can be received in relationships with our
fellow human beings."[89]

A major note in Meland's thought is the notion of dissonance which he
sees as implicit in the covenant relationship. The covenant relationship is only
valid if there is freedom on both sides, on the part of God and the individual
human. If the individual is free then there is the possibility of the individual
acting only in the interest of self without regard for the other center of
dignity, *i.e.*, God. When an individual does act only in the interest of self
then, according to Meland, the individual earns the name of sinner. This has
been symbolized in Christian thought as the "fall," or the rupturing of the
covenant relationship between individuals and God. The responsibility for
repairing the rupture is taken on by God, by a God who enters into the
finitude and conditionedness of human existence. Thus the events surrounding
Jesus, who was called the Christ, become a thematic way of speaking about
God's faithfulness in the covenant relationship in spite of the separation
caused by human obstinacy. The theme of the Suffering Servant reveals
"God's faithfulness at work in the covenant relationship, taking on the anguish
and burden of the relationship, both in its duration and in its brokenness."[90]
Meland sees this theme as originating in the Hebrew scriptures but, for him, it
takes on deeper significance "in the New Testament rendering of the work of
Christ as God taking on the form of man and reconciling the world to himself."[91]

Ontologically, Meland argues that the nature of God was not changed
by the historical event of Jesus as the Christ. "The energies of grace, I am
saying, antedate all Hebraic and Judaic structures. God was not rendered more
sensitive as saving love or as Suffering Servant by Jesus Christ; he was
disclosed as such."[92] What the image of Christ reveals from the point of view
of ontology "is that God is related to men, that He is concerned, that He is

involved in the turmoil and indecision of this troubled existence."[93] The image of the Christ asserts that "God suffers, as He suffered in Jesus Christ who died on the Cross."[94]

Meland goes on to point out that in the resurrection of Jesus Christ the Christian community has seen the continued faithfulness of God offering new hope for renewed grace and life within history.[95] The point I am making is that Meland images God as a particular individual relating to other individuals. God is seen, in the Christ figure, as a concrete individual relating to other individuals on a personal basis. Kaplan differs from Meland by envisioning God in terms of official function whereby God relates to the people as a whole and not to individuals. A king relates to a people by virtue of the office held. Meland's image of God as a first century Galilean emphasizes that an individual relates to other individuals on the basis of personal empathies and not on the basis of official function. Thus in the images which they present as indicative of the nature of God, Kaplan, true to what Lamprecht sees as Judaism's basic thrust, emphasizes images that stress the primacy of the "people," while Meland, in accordance with his Protestant heritage, emphasizes images that stress the importance of the individual.

1. Cf. Kaplan, *The Religion of Ethical Nationhood*, 7.

2. Kaplan, *Judaism without Supernaturalism*, 198.

3. Cf. Meland, *Fallible Forms*, 155–156.

4. Meland, *Faith and Culture*, 15.

5. Ibid., 16.

6. Ibid., 194.

7. Kaplan, *Religion of Ethical Nationhood*, 10.

8. Meland, "Mystic Returns," 17.

9. Ibid., 149.

10. Ibid., 157.

11. Meland, *Higher Education and Human Spirit*, 172.

12. Kaplan, *Religion of Ethical Nationhood*, 75.

13. Meland, *Faith and Culture*, 38.

14. Ibid., 85.

15. Meland, *Fallible Forms*, 141.

16. Kaplan, *Meaning of God*, 6.

17. Cf. Meland, *Fallible Forms*, 165, 176–177.

18. Kaplan, *Judaism as a Civilization*, 513.

19. Ibid.

20. Kaplan, *Religion of Ethical Nationhood*, 24.

21. Ibid.

22. Ibid., 25.

23. Kaplan, *Judaism as a Civilization*, 514.

24. Kaplan, *Judaism without Supernaturalism*, 198.

25. Ibid.

26. Ibid., 199.

27. Cf. Ibid., 106.

28. Ibid., 235.

29. Kaplan, *Meaning of God*, 9.

30. Ibid., 53.

31. Ibid.

32. Ibid., 53–54.

33. Meland, *Fallible Forms and Symbols*, 158.

34. Ibid., 168.

35. Meland, *Faith and Culture*, 198.

36. Kaplan, *Religion of Ethical Nationhood*, 10.

37. Cf. Kaplan *Judaism without Supernaturalism*, 34–35; Kaplan, *Questions Jews Ask*, 204–211; and Kaplan, *Future of the American Jew*, 211–219.

38. Kaplan, *Judaism as a Civilization*, 25.

39. Ibid., 255. For the complete discussion, ibid., 253–258.

40. Kaplan, *Meaning of God*, 6.

41. Cf. Kaplan *Judaism as a Civilization*, 156–158.

42. Ibid., 255.

43. Ibid., 258.

44. Cf. Ibid., 258–259.

45. Ibid., 259.

46. Ibid.

47. Cf. Ibid., 259–260.

48. Ibid., 260.

49. Jack J. Cohen, "Kaplan's Concept of Peoplehood," *Mordecai M. Kaplan: An Evaluation*. Eds. Ira Eisenstein and Eugene Kohn. (New York: Jewish Reconstructionist Foundation, 1952) 38.

50. Cf. Kaplan, *Judaism as a Civilization*, 261–263.

51. Kaplan, *Religion of Ethical Nationhood*, 10.

52. Ibid.; and cf. Kaplan, *Judaism without Supernaturalism*, 33–34. Also Kaplan, *Judaism as a Civilization*, 258–260.

53. Cf. Kaplan, *Questions Jews Ask*, 175, 210–211.

54. Kaplan, *Religion of Ethical Nationhood*, 139.

55. Meland, *Fallible Forms and Symbols*, 96.

56. Meland, *Realities of Faith*, 46.

57. Ibid., 47.

58. Ibid.

59. Ibid., 47–48.

60. Whitehead, Process and Reality, 410; cf. Ibid., 410-412.

61. Cf. Meland, *Faith and Culture*, 51–53; and Meland, *Realities of Faith*, 48.

62. Meland, *Faith and Culture*, 52.

63. Ibid., 51.

64. Meland, *Realities of Faith*, 47–48.

65. Ibid., 47.

66. Ibid.

67. Meland, *Faith and Culture*, 126–127.

68. Ibid., 127.

69. Ibid.

70. Kaplan, *Religion of Ethical Nationhood*, 6.

71. Ibid., 4, and cf. Kaplan, "The Sovereignty of God," *Reconstructionist* 31 (October 1, 1965): 9.

72. Kaplan, *Religion of Ethical Nationhood*, 51.

73. Kaplan, *Meaning in God*, 102.

74. Kaplan, *Meaning of God in Modern Jewish Religion*, 102.

75. Ibid., 108.

76. Ibid.

77. Ibid., 109.

78. Ibid., 110.

79. Ibid.

80. Ibid., 110–111.

81. Ibid., 119.

82. Ibid., 129.

83. Ibid.

84. Ibid., 135.

85. Cf. Daniel Liefer and Mordecai Kaplan, "Dialogue on Reconstructionism," *Reconstructionist* 29 (January 24, 1964): 8–10.

86. Meland, *Fallible Forms and Symbols*, 77.

87. Ibid.

88. Meland, *Realities of Faith*, 107.

89. Ibid.

90. Meland, *Fallible Forms and Symbols*, 99.

91. Ibid.

92. Meland, *Realities of Faith*, 181.

93. Ibid., 265.

94. Ibid.

95. Cf. Meland, *Fallible Forms and Symbols*, 100.

CHAPTER 5

THE FUTURE OF EMPIRICAL THEOLOGY

I do not wish to close this book without making some statement as to the future of Empirical Theology. Given the infinite number of variables and possibilities—and the quirk of human freedom—I hesitate to make firm predictions about any historical phenomenon. However, drawing on what we know of a given movement's past and present can give us some indications about its possible future. Therefore, before attempting to address the problem of the future direction of Empirical Theology we need to view the movement from a general philosophical and historical perspective.

We will begin by considering the question of methodology. To some extent the Empirical theologians are doing what any translator whose formative language is English does when she takes a text written in modern English and translates it into idiomatic, contemporary Chinese. The Empirical theologians are doing more than that, however, for the language into which they are translating the text is a language that shapes their own understanding of the way the world works. Empirical theologians share with other educated persons a common world view, a world view shaped, in part, by field theory and relativity in physics, by evolution in biology, by modern anthropology and sociological studies, and they are attempting to appropriate and reflect upon the insights and values of their religious traditions without denying the ways their mind-set has been shaped by the modern world view. Empirical theologians attempt to talk of meaning, justice, love and grace and the workings of God in the world in terms congruent with the modern world of thought which is also an ingredient of their own make-up. They are engaging in conversation both with other moderns and with the modernity of their own selves.

From the perspective of history, the kind of task the Empirical theologians are engaged in is not new. They are using the current idiom of their time to engage in conversation with the normative intellectuals of their day. It seems to me, then, that those engaged in Empirical Theology are doing in their day what Irenaeus, Clement of Alexandria, Origen and Maimonides did in theirs. The Empirical theologians are attempting, as did the early church theologians and Maimonides, to understand their religious faith within the normative, working, world view of the educated. One could argue that the Bible presents different cosmologies; the simple garden with four sides, representing the created world of the second chapter of Genesis, differs markedly from the cyclic view of the world found in Ecclesiastes and both of these differ from the world view with its seven levels of heavens of St. Paul in the Christian New Testament. When Aristotelianism was accepted as the explicator of all scientific thought, the scriptural text began to be interpreted through the eyes of Ptolemy. Leading church theologians as well as leading scientists from that time on until after the time of Copernicus accepted without question that the sun circled around the earth. Luther's strained exegesis of Joshua 10 could only have been enunciated by someone whose mind-set was already molded by the Aristotelian cosmology. The intelligentsia of Luther's day, not just the theologians but also the scientists, were convinced of the basic correctness of the Ptolemaic universe, just as any modern thinker, whether physicist or theologian, is convinced that the earth orbits around the sun and that the sun is just one of many orbiting bodies in the universe.

Copernicus' world view replaced Aristotle's or Ptolemy's because it was a theory which more elegantly or aesthetically made better sense out of the rapidly accumulating empirical data. In our day Einstein's theory of relativity made Newtonian physics obsolete; Einstein's theory made possible the inclusion of more of the data of physics and made the data fit more smoothly. In a like manner, Darwin's evolutionary reading made sense of the data of natural science in a way that Aristotelian biology with its doctrine of fixed species did not.

These shifts in understanding found in the natural sciences had repercussions in other fields. In theology, given the new dynamic, changing, understandings of the workings of the world, Aristotle's perfect-unmoving-square understanding of God no longer seemed, to many, to be adequate. For some theologians, Aristotle's picture of God was less adequate to deal with relativity theory, evolutionary theory in natural science, human experience, or with the picture of God provided by the Biblical text, than were theories such as Lloyd Morgan's and Alfred Whitehead's which allowed for change and experience to enter the life of God. These Empirical theologians engaged in a task which was important once the modern, scientific world view became pervasive for most intellectuals, not just scientists. These theologians were trying to discuss the meaning of their religious traditions within the sophisticated idiom of their day. It is a continuing task, a task which will need to be carried out in the future, whenever persons within a religious tradition find that the old comfortable modes in which its theological statements have been framed can no longer find a point of reference with the current world view of those on the forefront of scientific, philosophical and anthropological thinking.

As the normative world view changes for the intellectuals (including theologians) of a given day, the understanding of the way God works in the world also changes. Thus one cannot argue that Morgan or Whitehead have given us a final, definitive understanding of God's working in the world that will be valid for all ages and times to come, any more than one could assume that Einstein's theory of relativity or Stephen Hawking's self-enclosed, but unbounded universe, is the final word on the nature of the universe. At the same time, I am equally convinced that it is impossible for any enlightened scientist or theologian to return in any direct or simple fashion to a past picture of the universe, whether it be the modest, three story cosmology of the ancient, or to—from the perspectives of the ancients—the radical modern view of Ptolemy. To return to any past cosmological picture would only be possible if one could overlook the massive empirical data and the greater coherence of later theories.

A theologian of our day, who wishes to be heard by those on the forefront of science and culture who shape the way in which the world is understood, is obliged, it seems to me, to speak in terms that make sense to those to whom such a theologian wishes to speak. To speak out of a world view that is radically different means the theologian is either asking those who listen to compartmentalize their lives, making one truth, or way of understanding truth, acceptable in one sphere of the listener's life and another truth acceptable in other spheres; or the theologian is asking the listeners to abandon the current intellectual world altogether and withdraw into a strange world totally isolated from the world in which other moderns live. If the theologian has a strong regard for personal integrity, or wholeness, then the theologian is obliged to take seriously the world view and mind-set of the current culture. However, the theologian is never obliged to suppress or minimize the religious wisdom, the moral and aesthetic values and poetic images which a culture provides in the interest of being in agreement with any given, special scientific theory. The theologians task is to broaden and deepen our understanding of experience, not to truncate or narrow our understanding of experience.

At this point, in order to advance our understanding of the intellectual perspective of Empirical Theology, we need to look at some more of the basic assumptions shared by the empiricists. The Empirical theologians are not only translators from one way of speaking to another as was the case in regards to the English speaking person engaged in communicating to the Chinese, who we spoke about earlier in this chapter; the Empirical theologians are attempting to formulate a new language adequate to express the new insights of sciences such as physics in relation to their understanding of religion and God. They can neither simply fall back on the old traditional language of their respective religious traditions nor simply take over scientific terminology as adequate to express religious sensibilities. They have turned to philosophers who seek to make sense of the new understandings of science and add words such as "prehension" and "emergent" to their description of the way God works in the world. But even in its use of philosophy, the Empirical theologians cannot simply appropriate the terminology. The Empirical theologian has to formulate new terms, such as "the appreciative consciousness" in order to supplement philosophical and scientific language. The theologian formulates new expressions, analogous to philosophical and scientific ones, in order to emphasize the elements of grace and sin, the elements of individual responsibility in relation to God which the other sciences do not.

The Empirical theologians, as our Chinese translator may or may not be, are philosophical realists. They are realists in the sense of taking seriously that the relations which our general theories, arising out of the special sciences, attempt to express, describe (to some extent and in varying degrees) actual relations in the empirical situation. The empiricists insist that these general theories are not simply organizing pictures supplied by the mind. The person perceives actual, objective relations. There is no metaphysical split between knower and known, nor between noumena and phenomena. One of the appeals of Empirical Theology for me lies in the fact that my religious sensibilities are also in agreement with the above affirmation of the unity of experience, since I come out of a type of pietistic background which insisted that God's grace was part of the total empirical situation and which naively denied any separation between essence and act. This is why theologies which posit some form of split in reality—whether based on a split between spirit and matter, or based on a distinction between noumena and phenomena in the Kantian sense, or based on discrete areas of inquiry in the manner of logical positivism and language analysis—have never been, for me, intellectually or emotionally satisfying. Grace qualifies all of reality, not some section or dimension of reality.

Not only are Empirical theologians realists, they are also relativists. A relativist, whether a scientist or a theologian, assumes that any and every system of relations can be replaced by another system taking into account more of the relational data. Thus, in part, any new advance in theological systems, just as any advance in science or the arts, has to await new awareness of data, and a new synthesis or new way of seeing that data. Not that theology is simply bound to re-echo the findings or theories of any particular science, since for the theologian grace and goodness, as well as evil and destruction, are as indigenous to the empirical situation as are the data of physics and biology. The theologian needs to be peculiarly attentive to the cultural evidence of the relation of God and humankind, while accepting the evidences of the other sciences as supplying important modifications in that understanding of the relation between the divine and human. Because the Empirical theologian takes seriously both the need to strive for wholeness, and the need to be open and responsive to the world, the theologian can never be satisfied with theological formulations applicable to a past age which are no longer relevant, nor can the theologian be satisfied that the present system, whatever form it happens to take, will be applicable to future situations. Thus I view with some alarm the tendency of those I have called the rationalists in the Empirical Movement to overemphasize structure and coherence at the expense of perception, at the expense of remaining open to the seeming, chaotic flux of experience. An overemphasis on logical categories can prevent the seeing of parts of the relational flux that do not fit the schema and it can prevent the seeking of new ways of apprehending that flux. Like the new scientists whom James Gleick, describes who are as much intrigued by randomness and complexity as by order and simplicity, the theologian is ever seeking for new ways to describe order and chaos, determinism and indeterminism, and individual responses that much of traditional and modern science has overlooked.

The notion of relativity has another aspect. I am enough of a mystical poet to suggest that while we may indeed come close to discovering something of the mind of God in relation to the past, whether of the creation of our universe, à la Stephen Hawkings, or of the creation of myriads of other such universes, and while we may come closer to discovering something of the mind of God in relation to present perceptions of goodness, God in joyful exuberance and with cheerful good humor may be evolving new and different variations and systems that go far beyond our limited grasps. Even as we evolve as a species into more and more knowledgeable beings, we may be involved in a race in which we can never catch-up. As we change God is also changing, making whatever we know of the divine existence always partial and incomplete.

Flights of fancy aside, but taking into consideration the intellectual and historical reasons for the emergence of the Empirical movement in theology, and the movement's persistent attraction for many, I can now offer suggestions as to the direction Empirical Theology needs to go if it is to continue to be a vital force in the future. The program for Empirical Theology, if it is to remain a vital movement, is to submerge itself ever more deeply in the empirical data; to be open to new theories in physics, natural science, biology and the human sciences, without ignoring the imaginative, emotive, poetic, and individual aspects of our existence. By being open to the relational flux of human experience, Empirical theologians may be able to aid the coming "modern" person to achieve a better understanding of the workings of God in the universe and in the "modern" person's life. What future Empirical theologians can learn from present day empiricists such as Kaplan and Meland is to take seriously both their special religious traditions and the total world in which they find themselves. Future Empirical theologians need to value their own past and the peculiar, religious tradition that nurtured them, while being open to the complexity and multi-dimensionality of the world of which they are a part. As long as the world and our perception of it changes, there will be a need for those who attempt to carry on the theological task in the empirical mode.

On the programmatic level, if Empirical Theology is to survive and recruit new members into its fold, its adherents need to focus on writing clear statements about its origins and basic orientation that are intelligible to the educated non-specialist. Some of the impact that Barth and Brunner had on the American educational scene can be traced to the fact that their followers made their ideas accessible to the general reader. If Empirical Theology is to have a similar impact, it too must produce works aimed at the non-specialist and the theological beginner. Empirical Theology should not be ignored or rejected simply because it is not understood. Indeed, I was prompted to write this book by my concern to make this movement more accessible to the general reader in theology.

BIBLIOGRAPHY

Works of Mordecai M. Kaplan

"An Antidote to Jewish Anti-Semitism." *SAJ Review* 6 (March 25, 1927): 5–12.

"Aspirations and Handicaps of the Zionist Organization of America." *SAJ Review* 8 (October 19, 1928): 10–17.

"Can Zionism Reconstitute the Jewish People?" *The Reconstructionist* 29 (October 4, 1963): 6–15.

"The Chosen People Idea: an Anachronism." *The Reconstructionist* 11 (January 11, 1946): 13–19.

"Critique of the Adjustment of Reform." *SAJ Review* 8 (March 22, 1929): 21–23.

"Critique of the Adjustment of Orthodoxy." *SAJ Review* 8 (March 8, 1929): 11–19.

"Emancipation or Redemption—Which?" *SAJ Review* 8 (April 4, 1928): 4–8.

"The Future of Judaism." *The Menorah Journal* 2 (June 1916): 160–172.

The Future of the American Jew. New York: Macmillan Co., 1948.

"The God Idea in the Problem of Revaluation." *SAJ Review* 8 (October 12, 1928): 8–18.

"A God to Match the Universe." *The Reconstructionist* 23 (March 19, 1965): 22–27.

Ed. with Ira Eisenstein and Eugene Kohn. *High Holiday Prayer Book*, vol. 1. New York: Jewish Reconstructionist Foundation, Inc., 1948.

"How May Judaism be Saved?" *The Menorah Journal* 2 (February 1916): 34–44.

"The Influences that have Shaped my Life." *The Reconstructionist* 8 (June 15, 1942): 26–35.

Judaism as a Civilization. Philadelphia: Reconstructionist Press, 1937.

"Judaism as a Civilization." *SAJ Review* 8 (March 29, 1929): 13–22.

"Judaism's Adjustment to the Environment." *SAJ Review* 8 (March 2, 1929): 10–24.

"Judaism as an Unconscious Evolution." *SAJ Review* 7 (March 30, 1928): 9–16.

Judaism without Supernaturalism. New York: Reconstructionist Press, 1958.

"The Law of Group Survival as Applied to the Jews." *SAJ Review* 8 (September 21, 1928): 237–239.

The Meaning of God in Modern Jewish Religion. New York: Reconstructionist Press, 1962.

"Nationhood the Call of the Spirit." *SAJ Review* 8 (May 24, 1929): 12–20.

The Nationhood of Israel." *SAJ Review* 8 (May 17, 1929): 13–24.

"Naturalism as a Source of Morality and Religion." *The Reconstructionist* 29 (February 22, 1963): 11–16.

"On Creeds and Wants." *The Menorah Journal* 21 (April–June 1933): 33–52.

"Paradox—as Witness of the Spiritual." *SAJ Review* 6 (April 1, 1929): 5–11.

Questions Jews Ask. New York: Reconstructionist Press, 1956.

"The Relation of Religion to Civilization." *SAJ Review* 8 (April 12, 1929): 8–23.

The Religion of Ethical Nationhood. New York: The Macmillan Company, 1970.

"A Reply." *SAJ Review* 8 (February 1, 1929): 10–15.

"The Revaluation of the Concept Torah." *SAJ Review* 8 (May 13, 1929): 9–19.

"Revaluation of Jewish Values." *SAJ Review* 8 (September 28, 1928): 4–12.

"The Sovereignty of God." *The Reconstructionist* 31 (October 1, 1965): 7–13.

"Spiritual Leaders for our Day." *The Reconstructionist* 34 (November 8, 1968): 7–10.

"The Way I have Come." *Mordecai M. Kaplan: An Evaluation,* 283–321. Eds. Eugene Kohn and Ira Eisenstein. New York: Jewish Reconstructionist Foundation, Inc., 1948.

Works of Bernard E. Meland

With Henry Nelson Wieman. *American Philosophies of Religion.* Chicago: Willett, Clark and Co., 1936.

"Analogy and Myth in Post Liberal Theology." *Process Philosophy and Christian Thought,* 116–127. Eds. Delwin Brown, Ralph E. James, Jr., and Gene Reeves. New York: Bobs-Merrill Co., Inc., 1971.

"The Appreciative Approach in Religion." *The Journal of Religion* 14 (1934): 194–204.

"Can Empirical Theology Learn From Phenomenology?" *The Future of Empirical Theology,* 283–306. Ed. Bernard E. Meland. Chicago: University of Chicago Press, 1969.

"Chicago School of Theology," *Encyclopedia of Religious Knowledge,* vol. 1, 232–233. Grand Rapids, MI: Baker Book House, 1955.

"Education for a Spiritual Culture." *The Journal of Religion* 26 (1946): 87–100.

"The Empirical Tradition in Theology at Chicago." *The Future of Empirical Theology*, 1–62. Ed. Bernard E. Meland. Chicago: The University of Chicago Press, 1969.

"From Darwin to Whitehead: A Study in the Shift in Ethos and Perspective Underlying Religious Thought." *The Journal of Religion* 40 (October 1960): 229–245.

Faith and Culture. New York: Oxford University Press, 1953; London: George Allen and Unwin, 1955.

Fallible Forms and Symbols. Philadelphia: Fortress Press, 1976.

"The Genius of Protestantism." *The Journal of Religion* 27 (1947): 273–292.

"Grace: A Dimension within Nature?" *The Journal of Religion* 54 (1974): 119–137.

Higher Education and the Human Spirit. Chicago: University of Chicago Press, 1953.

"How is Culture a Source for Theology?" *Criterion* 3 (1964): 10–21.

"In Response to Frankenberry." *American Journal of Theology and Philosophy* 5 (May and September, 1981): 130–137.

"In Response to Loomer." *American Journal of Theology and Philosophy* 5 (May and September, 1981): 144–155.

"In Response to Miller." *American Journal of Theology and Philosophy* 5 (May and September, 1981): 107–116.

"Interpreting the Christian Faith within a Philosophical Framework." *The Journal of Religion* 33 (April 1953): 87–102.

"Is God Many or One?" *The Christian Century* 24 (1933): 725–726.

Modern Man's Worship. New York: Harper and Bros., 1934.

"The Mystic Returns." *The Journal of Religion* (1937): 147–160.

"New Dimensions of Liberal Faith." *The Christian Century* 74 (1957): 961–963.

"The Present Issue in Christianity." *The Christian Century* 56 (February 1, 1939): 156–157.

Realities of Faith. New York: Oxford University Press, 1962.

The Reawakening of Christian Faith. New York: The Macmillan Co., 1949.

"Reflections on the Early Chicago School of Modernism," *American Journal of Theology and Philosophy* 5 (January 1984): 3–12.

"Religion has Not Lost its Hold." *Religious Education* 21 (July 1935): 26–30.

Seeds of Redemption. New York: The Macmillan co., 1947.

"Seeing God in Human Life." *The Christian Century* 53 (1936): 490–492.

The Secularization of Modern Culture. New York: Oxford University Press, 1966.

"Some Unresolved Issues in Theology." *The Journal of Religion* 24 (1944): 233–239.

"Theology and the Historian of Religion." *The Journal of Religion* 41 (1961): 263–276.

"Toward a Common Christian Faith." *Christendom* 1 (1937): 388–399.

"Toward a Valid View of God." *Harvard Theological Review* 24 (1931): 197–208.

"Why Religion?" *The Methodist Quarterly Review* 79 (1930): 359–362.

Selected References

Agus, Jacob B. "God in Kaplan's Philosophy." *Judaism* 30 (Winter 1981): 30–35.

Ahad Ha-Am. "Many Inventions." *Selected Essays of Ahad Ha-Am*. 165–167. Ed. and trans. Leon Simon. New York: Atheneum, 1970.

_____. "Priest and Prophet." *Selected Essays of Ahad Ha–Am*. 132–133. Ed. and trans. Leon Simon. New York: Atheneum, 1970.

_____. "The Spiritual Revival." *Selected Essays of Ahad Ha-Am*, 262–263. Ed. and trans. Leon Simon. New York: Atheneum, 1970.

_____. "Three Steps." *Sources of Contemporary Jewish Thought*, no. 1, 53–54. Ed. David Harden. Jerusalem: World Zionist Organization, 1970.

Axel, Larry E. "The Chicago School of Theology and Henry Nelson Wieman." *Encounter* 40 (Autumn 1979): 341–358.

_____. "The Root and Form of Meland's Elementalism." *Journal of Religion* 60 (October 1980): 472–490.

Barbour, Ian G. *Issues in Science and Religion*. Englewood Cliffs, NJ: Prentice-Hall, Inc., 1966.

_____. *Myths, Models, and Paradigms: A Comparative Study in Science and Religion*. New York: Harper and Row, Publishers, 1974.

Berkovits, Eliezer. *Modern Themes in Modern Philosophies of Judaism*. New York: KTAV Publishing House, Inc., 1974.

Blumenfield, Samuel M. "Mordecai M. Kaplan—Ahad Ha-Am of American Jewry." *The Reconstructionist* 22 (April 20, 1956): 8–13.

Brown, Delwin and Gene Reeves. "The Development of Process Theology," *Process Philosophy and Christian Thought*, 23–69. Eds. Delwin Brown, Ralph E. James, Jr., and Gene Reeves. New York: Bobbs-Merrill Co., Inc., 1971.

Browning, Don. *Pluralism and Personality.* Cranbury, NJ: Associated University Presses, Inc., 1980.

Bultmann, Rudolf. *Kerygma and Myth.* New York: Harper Torchbooks, 1961.

Cobb, John B. *Living Options in Protestant Theology.* Philadelphia: The Westminster Press, 1962.

Cohen, Arthur A. and Mordecai Kaplan. *If not Now, When?* New York: Schocken Books, 1973.

Cohen, Jack J. "Kaplan's Concept of Peoplehood." *Mordecai M. Kaplan: An Evaluation*, 27–44. Eds. Ira Eisenstein and Eugene Kohn. New York: Jewish Reconstructionist Foundation, 1952.

Davis, Moshe. *The Emergence of Conservative Judaism.* Philadelphia: The Publication Society of America, 1963.

Dean, William. "Radical Empiricism and Religious Art." *Journal of Religion* 61 (April 1981): 168–187.

Dewey, John. *A Common Faith.* New Haven: Yale University Press, 1934.

_____. *Experience and Nature.* Chicago: Open Court Publishing Co., 1929.

_____. *The Quest for Certainty.* New York: G.P. Putnam's Sons, 1929.

_____. *Reconstruction in Philosophy.* New York: A Mentor Book, The New American Library, 1920.

_____. *Individualism Old and New.* New York: Capricorn Books, 1929.

Dinn, Samuel. "Organic Jewish Community." *Mordecai M. Kaplan: An Evaluation*, 45–64. Eds. Ira Eisenstein and Eugene Kohn. New York: Jewish Reconstructionist Foundation, 1952.

Durkheim, Emile. *The Elementary Forms of Religious Life.* New York: The Free Press, 1915.

234 The American Empirical Movement in Theology

Frankenberry, Nancy. "Meland's Empirical Realism and the Appeal to Lived Experience." *American Journal of Theology and Philosophy* 5 (May and September 1981): 117–129.

Gleick, James. *Chaos: Making a New Science.* New York: Penguin Paperback, 1988.

Hartshorne, Charles. *The Logic of Perfection.* LaSalle, IL: Open Court Publishing Co., 1964.

_____. *Man's Vision of God.* Hamden, CT: Archon Books, 1964.

Hawking, Stephen M. *A Brief History of Time from the Big Bang to Black Holes.* New York: Bantam Books, 1988.

Heschel, Abraham Joshua. "The Spirit of Jewish Prayer." *R.A. Proceedings* 17 (1953): 162–163.

Hume, David. *An Enquiry Concerning Human Understanding.* Section 7, Parts 1 and 2. Ed. L.A. Selby-Bigge. Oxford: Oxford Clarendon Press, 1894–96.

Inbody, Ty. "Bernard Meland: A Rebel Among Process Theologians." *American Journal of Theology and Philosophy* 5 (May and September, 1981): 43–71.

James, William. *Collected Essays and Reviews.* Ed. R. B. Perry. New York: Longmans Green and Co., 1911.

_____. *Essays on Faith and Morals.* New York: Meridian Books, The World Publishing Co., 1962.

_____. *A Pluralistic Universe.* New York: Longmans, 1911.

_____. *Pragmatism.* London: Longmans, Green and Co., 1928.

_____. *The Principles of Psychology*, 2 volumes. New York: Dover Publications, Inc., 1890.

_____. *Varieties of Religious Experience.* New York: Mentor Books, 1902.

_____. *The Will to Believe and Other Essays in Popular Philosophy and Human Immortality*. New York: Dover Publications, 1956

_____. *The Writings of William James*. Ed. John McDermott. New York: The Modern Library, 1968.

Janzen, Gerald J. "Meland as Yahwistic Theologian of Culture." *The Journal of Religion* 60 (October 1980): 391–410.

Kaufman, William E. *Contemporary Jewish Philosophies*. New York: Jewish Reconstructionist Press, 1976.

Kohs, Samuel C. "Jewish Social Work." *Mordecai M. Kaplan: An Evaluation*, 65–87. Eds. Ira Eisenstein and Eugene Kohn. New York: Jewish Reconstructionist Foundation, 1952.

Kraft, Louis. "The Jewish Center Movement." *Mordecai M. Kaplan: An Evaluation*, 119–146. Eds. Ira Eisenstein and Eugene Kohn. New York: Jewish Reconstructionist Foundation, 1952.

Kuhn, Thomas S. *The Structure of Scientific Revolutions*. Chicago: The University of Chicago Press, 1962.

Lamprecht, Sterling P. *Our Religious Tradition*. Cambridge: Harvard University Press, 1950.

Leifer, Daniel and Mordecai Kaplan. "Dialogue on Reconstructionism." *The Reconstructionist* 29 (January 24, 1964): 6–15.

Libowitz, Richard. *Mordecai M. Kaplan and the Development of Reconstructionism*. New York: The Edwin Mellon Press, 1963.

Loomer, Bernard M. "Empirical Theology within Process Thought." *The Future of Empirical Theology*, 151–158. Ed. Bernard E. Meland. Chicago: University of Chicago Press, 1969.

Lor, Aaron Arieh. "Process in Judaism." California Institute of Asian Studies, unpublished, 1975.

Miller, Randolph Crump. *The American Spirit in Theology*. Philadelphia: United Church Press, 1974.

Parzen, Herbert. *Architects of Conservative Judaism.* New York: Jonathan David, 1964.

Polish, David. "Jewish Liturgy." *Mordecai M. Kaplan: An Evaluation*, 211–222. Eds. Ira Eisenstein and Eugene Kohn. New York: Jewish Reconstructionist Foundation, 1952.

Saltzer, Robert M. *Jewish People, Jewish Thought.* New York: The Macmillan Co., Inc., 1980.

Simon, Leon. *Ahad Ha-Am.* Philadelphia: The Jewish Publication Society of America, 1960.

Smith, Gerald Birney. "The Nature of Science and of Religion and their Interpretation." *Religious Education* 23 (1919): 308–310.

_____. "Is Theism Essential to Theology?" *American Journal of Theology* 24 (January 1920): 153–154.

_____. "Religious Experience and Scientific Method." *Journal of Religion* 6 (1936): 38–64.

Seltzer, David. *The Jewish Experience in History.* New York: Macmillan Publishing Co., Inc., 1980.

Whitehead, Alfred North. *Adventures of Ideas.* New York: The Macmillan Co., 1933.

_____. *Process and Reality.* New York: The Free press, 1929.

Wieman, Henry Nelson. *Intellectual Foundations of Faith.* New York: Philosophical Library, Inc., 1961.

_____. *Man's Ultimate Commitment.* Carbondale, IL: Southern Illinois University Press, 1958.

_____. "Mordecai M. Kaplan's Idea of God." *Mordecai M. Kaplan: An Evaluation*, 193–210. Eds. Ira Eisenstein and Eugene Kohn. New York: Jewish Reconstructionist Foundation, 1952.

_____. *The Source of Human Good.* Carbondale, IL: Southern Illinois University Press, 1946.

INDEX